Animal Prints
on My
Soul

Animal Prints
on My
Soul

Candace Gish

a Divas
That Care
Collection

Absolute Love Publishing

Absolute Love Publishing
Animal Prints on My Soul

Published by Absolute Love Publishing
USA

Cover photo by Werner Images

ISBN-13: 979-8-9855746-0-9

United States of America

By Candace Gish
Animal Prints on My Soul

Dedication ♡

To all the animals that have influenced my life over the years, and the ones yet to come.

Table of Contents

HEALING

CONNECTION

LOVE AND LOSS

CONTRIBUTOR BIOS

Healing

"The wound is the place where the Light enters you."
~ Rumi

When we think of animals, we often think in terms of companionship but not always in terms of reducing our stress and anxiety or increasing our playfulness. Yet, animals have an amazing ability to be exactly what we need them to be.

I have always had a lot of animals in my life, but for many years I never thought about how these animals might be healing me. This changed when I was in my 20's and on the other side of a bad relationship. It took me time to realize it, but I had become a shell of the person I used to be. Then, I met an amazing Great Dane puppy who happened to be deaf. He changed everything. I devoted so much time to him, teaching him sign language and going to agility classes. What I didn't realize until later was that by focusing on loving him, I started to heal myself. He loved me unconditionally through every moment and eventually taught me how to love again.

Sometimes, animals come into our lives for a greater purpose than we realize. The unconditional love they give comforts and supports us – and in many cases, also heals us. These stories of healing are such a joy and show us how animals can be the perfect blessing for our lives at the perfect time.

The Wisdom of Horses

Angie Payne

I have been fortunate to have had horses in my life since I was 13 years old, when I carried the belief that I saved a horse's life! As I look back, I realize it wasn't me helping horses, but them helping me, since they have held me at different moments in my life. As I write this story, I am in my sixties. This is a long time to have been in relationship with these incredible beings, and I feel blessed to have had their continual guidance and ability to challenge me.

In my early teens, I experienced a sexual assault. At that tender age I didn't know what to do with the experience. Sexual assault wasn't something freely talked about, so I kept it to myself until I was in my fifties. Feeling like I had to keep it a secret changed the course of my life. I'm a sensitive person, and the pain and trauma of that experience sat in my body for a very long time.

During the aftermath, I had a horse who wasn't doing well, either, so I took it upon myself to give him the will to live. And while I thought I was healing him, he was actually healing me. This was the horse that helped me stay on the planet.

The opportunity to care for that horse brought me out of some pretty dark places. I know I decided to stay on this planet because of him. I can recall moments of crying into his mane while he stood perfectly still, holding space, and I felt safe to allow the tears to flow. We would often go riding together for hours. It was the solitude and knowing I was safe, heard, and seen on those days together that saved me from my past. I will always be grateful for that beautiful being and his ability to keep me safe even when we found ourselves in tricky situations. While I was able to express my emotions to him, I wasn't aware that what I had experienced was trauma I would struggle with for a long time. I did my best to keep my head above water and avoid depression, but, unfortunately, not talking about the sexual assault affected every relationship I had. As I look back, I realize I didn't feel worthy, or of value, which made me sabotage the good in my life.

At the age of 24, I became pregnant with my first child, and I couldn't have been happier. At that time, I was still finding solitude and safety with horses. I had three horses that brought me joy and a reoccurring feeling of safety and security when I was in their presence. During those early stages of pregnancy, I had many different emotions I couldn't understand. I was still unaware of how the earlier experience of sexual assault had impacted me and my relationships.

I was four-and-a-half months pregnant when I lost my baby. I felt like nobody really understood, but for me, the loss, grief, and despair were so real. I really didn't know what to do with the emotions I had, so I simply moved on. My husband at the time and I never spoke about the incredible sadness this loss had caused, and our life went on. I again found myself going to the horses, where I knew my sorrow would be honored. I could recognize the pain, hold space for my emotions, and allow it to leave my body. Those three horses would wrap themselves around me, keeping me safe from the outside world. My husband and I tried time and time again to become pregnant, only to discover I couldn't have biological children. I was devastated because I had held onto the idea that this was what I wanted most of all. Instead of dealing with the loss, I again moved on, never realizing it was all just piling up inside of me.

Horses have held space for me at the lowest of times and have also been with me during the happiest of times. In 1986, I finally got what I had always wanted. We welcomed a beautiful little girl into our lives through adoption. I remember taking my baby girl out to the horses because, of course, they would want to meet her. They put their big, yet tender muzzles on that little being as if they were checking her out, and I believe they were telling her they would keep her safe as they did me. I felt like I was the luckiest person in the world.

The unrecognized trauma and the troll on my shoulder were still there, though, and at this stage in my life, they felt too heavy. The belief that I was not worthy or enough reared its ugly head again. When my marriage ended, I found myself a single mom, paying the bills and providing for my daughter. Because of this change, horses no longer fit into my tight budget and so they disappeared from my life. Life got crazy and, reflecting now, I know that I would come to a place where I would not be able to hold the pain and trauma. My body was screaming at me, and I just couldn't listen. I couldn't look at the deep pain of my life.

I've learned it's only when we are ready to drop our walls that healing can really begin. It's a place of vulnerability that we must be prepared to face, and it's complicated. The walls drove my bus for a couple of years, and at times, I felt totally out of control because I didn't have horses to regulate my emotions. My little girl and I were left to find our way in the world, and we had many joyful moments. Yet, I struggled with my emotions and self-sabotaging behaviors I couldn't recognize at the time. I was white-knuckling it through life, trying my best to be what I needed to be for my daughter, my (later) new husband, my job, and my friends. Still, something was not right. I was numb and I was scared. Scared to be vulnerable, scared to be weak, scared to trust, scared of the world and life. Emotionally, I had very little control, and I still had no understanding of why I was feeling this way.

When my beautiful daughter turned 13, she desired to have a horse. My heart skipped a beat, and I found myself excited about the prospect of her being able to experience the things I had. These horses had blessed me, and I wondered if they would impact her life like they had mine. I was elated that she would have a friend that could be present for her. To me, that was the most important gift I could give her. We managed to find a lovely horse, a perfect first partner. The horse was named Tia, and with her came an unborn baby. My daughter and Tia developed a loving and trusting relationship. It seemed that my daughter enjoyed horses and what they brought into her life. However, the deep love for horses that I had wasn't there for my daughter. Other passions emerged for her, and I knew that a relationship with horses couldn't be forced. As her mom, I watched her discover her new passions and supported her completely. The baby was born, and he has been a blessing in my life since 1999. My daughter named him Romeo.

The first four years of our time together, I found myself as his nursemaid. He was mostly either ill or injured, meaning he required continual care from me. I recognized that having a scared horse and an afraid human generally isn't a good combination. Caring for this young horse I learned to control my emotions and find a space of strength for my horse and myself.

Romeo and I created a strong relationship, and while that relationship was developing, I decided to find a way to be a better rider. I found a horseman whose philosophies around horses resonated with me, and Romeo and I started our journey together.

I learned that Romeo is a confident horse who knows what he wants and how to make the human in his life get those things. Little did I know that caring for Romeo was going to be the ride of my life, a ride that taught me how to ground and regulate myself. As Romeo became healthy, we started learning from the young horseman. I discovered that the journey was more than becoming a better rider; I was learning about how I was showing up in the world. Most of the time, with horses, if you are not acknowledging what they already know about you, they have difficulty connecting with you. Romeo helped me realize that I deeply desired connection, I just didn't know how to open myself up to it. The great thing about horses is they hold absolutely no judgement around any part of us. Horses can stand in compassion and can hold space no matter which emotion the human presents, as long as it is authentic.

One day I was riding Romeo, and the young horseman asked me a question. Romeo acted out something that appeared unique to me. I can't remember the details, but at that moment, what felt like a million puzzle pieces fell out of me, and I cried for what seemed like a lifetime. It felt like my entire life flooded out of me. Every emotion and the deep despair I had carried for so long broke the wall I had built, and I felt raw. I learned that day that once that happens, you can't put it back inside. You can't look away, and you can no longer cover it up. As I sat on Romeo crying, he was as still as a statue, holding me safely and experiencing everything that was happening. Not one muscle moved in his body for what seemed to be a long time. I believe Romeo would have stood there for a lifetime if that is what I had needed. Today, although I did not understand what was happening, I am grateful for that moment. That moment took me on a journey to learn how horses can support people who struggle with sadness, trauma, grief, despair, depression, and anxiety.

That transformational moment led me to seek out a psychologist and some horses for myself and spend two years peeling back the layers, exposing the pain that prevented me from living the happy, joyous life I desired. The hardest part was when that horse showed me something I needed to acknowledge, feel, and do the work to heal. Horses express their intuition without apology. They can undoubtedly act out scenarios that a human would not be able to. Horses bring us to our body, where trauma is held and where trauma must heal. The work was challenging, yet I wouldn't change a single thing. Romeo and that moment allowed me to find my passion and purpose on this planet. That moment also taught me that I needed my own support and guidance to process the trauma I had experienced in life.

As I think about my story, I wonder if I had written it years ago, would I be feeling the shame I had once carried? Romeo has taught me so much. I have learned how to be present, honor my feelings, and speak my truth when necessary. I also recognize that I need to tell my truth with love and compassion. I have learned that I am worthy of taking up space, and I have learned how to connect with others and myself. I have learned about healthy boundaries and how important they are to deepen relationships. I have learned I have a right to express my voice.

Sometimes I wish I had learned these things when I was young, but I hope now that I can inspire other women to use their voice and know they can take up space in this world. I am often reminded that healing is about having compassion for myself and making heartfelt and humble apologies when needed. Recovery is about moving in the world differently to find our hearts and share them with others. Opening up means there is a potential to be hurt, but learning to love and risking heartache, instead of never being open enough to experience love and connection, would be a significant loss. Along the way, I have been grateful to have wonderful mentors in my life, but most importantly, I thank the horses that have had my back along this journey called life.

Whispers from an Angel
Daphne McDonagh

Growing up in the country gave me many opportunities to be around animals, and I thought it was normal that I could hear what they were saying. It never even crossed my mind that others were not able to do the same.

There are many stories I could share, but for the purposes of this book I am going to tell you the journey I had with Shylo for 13 years of my married life. My family and I had just gone through the letting go of our dear blue heeler, Bandit, who had been full of cancer, when the opportunity arose for us to go to a friend's place and see some border collie puppies.

Our hearts were still broken from having to put Bandit down, and I did not want any part in getting a new puppy. But I was outvoted by my husband and our six-year-old son, and they came home with a beautiful little ball of fur that was so timid my husband had to crawl under the deck to retrieve her.

Choosing her name came easy, and Shylo became a part of our family. For the first year of her life, I really did not pay much attention to her as I was working hard to not fall in love with her like I had with Bandit. I knew that eventually she would also leave. Growing up in the country, this was a fact of life I was aware would happen, and I did not want to go through that pain again.

Shylo had such a gentle soul and was so patient with me. She stood beside me as I walked through many transitions in my life and never asked for a thing. It did not matter to her if I was overjoyed or sad, Shylo would simply sit beside me and unconditionally love me through thick and thin.

When I made the transition from working in a bank to doing rehabilitation treatments on animals and people, she started to talk to me. The first thing I can remember her saying was, "Finally, now you are ready to hear me." Little did I know she had been waiting to step into the role of a therapy dog. Shylo explained to me that I did not need to do this alone, and she was here to help me help others.

Her gentle and peaceful soul warmed the hearts of many people. I truly am forever grateful for her being a part of our family for so many years and helping so many people. It was really cute how she would tell me what was going on with someone before they would. She had an amazing way of simply coming and sitting beside whomever I was working with, and you could see their energy shift as soon as they touched her. Shylo was definitely an earth angel that came into our lives at the perfect time to assist me shifting into the next phase of my life.

Just over a year ago, we were given the chance to get a Lab puppy whose parents are hunting dogs. It was an opportunity we couldn't pass up, as my husband had always wanted a waterfowl hunting dog, and being that Shylo was not only terrified of guns but getting up there in years, we said yes and welcomed Gunner into our family.

It was so cute watching them together. She was definitely the big sister who watched out for her little brother and, at the same time, gave him heck for being so silly. Shylo would come to me and ask me to take him away because he was driving her nuts, but I knew deep down she loved him just as much as she loved us.

At the beginning of December of that year we started to notice her health deteriorating, but she would not tell me what was going on. I watched her slow down and start to lose her footing when she was trying to walk. But still, she would not let me know what was happening other than it was something in her head. She knew I was helping so many other animals and people, and she didn't want to worry me with what she was dealing with. It got to the point where I had to ask my friend Sheena to talk with her because she was not letting me in anymore. So off to the vet we went. The prognosis was a horrible ear infection and possibly a tumor on her brain.

The vet's office wanted us to do rounds of antibiotics for the ear infection and see how things fared. We chose not to do the test for the brain tumor because even if there was one, surgery would be very risky. Watching her slowly deteriorate in front of our eyes was one of the most heartbreaking experiences I have ever faced. It got to the point we had to pick her up to carry her outside to go to the bathroom.

It was then we made the hard decision to have her put down. When I asked her if she wanted us to keep trying options to help her regain her health, she told me, "I am good. Please allow me to go." I called and made the appointment to have her put down on December 21, 2020, which happened to be Winter Solstice.

I explained to her that she was welcome to go to sleep and just not wake up, but she explained to me that she did not want to do that to my husband or my son. She said it would be too traumatic for them. We would have to deal with her body, and she didn't want that. She was always thinking about others.

The morning of December 21, my husband, Shylo, and I went off to the vet clinic with Shylo and myself riding in the backseat. I again explained to her that she was okay to let go, and she refused. We stopped and got her one last treat just before taking her into the clinic, and as my husband tried to give it to her, she stood up and started to seizure. My husband jumped out of the front seat and helped me to get her out of the backseat as she continued to seizure, which inadvertently got us in the clinic way faster. I asked her why she chose to do that, and she said, "So Dad knows I am ready." She wanted him to know it was her time, and this was the best way she knew how.

Shylo was cremated on Christmas Eve. The day is so fitting for our beautiful angel. My parents also had a special place in their hearts for Shylo so they purchased a life-sized ceramic statue of a border collie. My mom then proceeded to paint Shylo's markings on the statue so that it looked like her. We couldn't think of a better day than June 21, 2021, to lay her to rest at the farm, which is not only the Summer Solstice but my husband's birthday. Her ashes were placed in the ground, and her statue sits on top of where she rests.

It truly is amazing how animals can come into our lives and how they touch our hearts so deeply. I feel so blessed and grateful to have been able to spend almost 13 full years with Shylo in our lives.

My Healing Journey with Animals

Diane Rose-Solomon

When I was a little girl, I was bullied a lot. I was small, sweet, naive, and an easy target. In middle school, in addition to taunting, the big, tough girls threatened to beat me up. It was scary, and I didn't have the emotional tools to deal with it. Who does?

I thought ... What did I do to deserve this? Will I survive? It didn't seem like anyone quite understood the torture. I know middle school can be tough for almost everyone. I also know my experience was painful.

So, I cried when I got home. And listened to music. And told my cat, Kougle, everything. He understood. He would wait under my bed for me every day after school, willing to listen and be with me. It was his honor and duty, and he loved his job. I know this because he was there for me every day, purring whenever we were together and sleeping on my pillow. Somehow, I'd manage to be just okay enough the next morning to get myself back to school.

He didn't care that I didn't have the right things to say back to the bullies, or that I said and did stupid stuff ALL THE TIME trying to be accepted. He just loved me for me. He was grateful for the warm home, attention, food, and love I gave him.

Obviously, I survived middle school, and I am forever grateful to Kougle. After college, I adopted a kitten my sister couldn't keep (she now fosters kittens) and named her Stevie. While not as dramatic, when I moved to Los Angeles from New York City in 1991, I left behind all my friends and family. I traveled with my cat, Stevie, and my boyfriend (now husband), and I adopted another cat named Rocky, whom we adored. Both cats were our constant companions.

But it was our first dog, JJ, who we accidentally rescued in 1995, who opened my eyes to the powers of animal rescue and adoption. JJ was also the gateway for me to meet neighbors and make friends while out on a walk. Most importantly, it was through JJ that I really fell in love with dogs and experienced for myself their loyalty and unconditional love.

During those early days with JJ, I got more involved with animal rescue and served on the board of directors of a small animal welfare organization, The Animal Guardian Society. Ultimately, we adopted other dogs, including T-bone, Ninja, and Gonzo.

Fast forward to 2009. My kids got the flu, then I got the flu, then they got better, and I didn't. I landed in the hospital with pneumonia. Around day four in the hospital, the infectious disease specialists came in because I was not responding to treatment. That same day (I think, though I couldn't be sure because I had a pretty high fever), a woman showed up at my hospital room door and asked if I wanted a visit from a dog.

"A dog? Of course!" I had no idea dogs were even allowed in hospitals.

She spread a clean sheet on my bed and up jumped Max. We visited for a few minutes, then Max left with his handler to visit another patient. Boy, did that visit lift my spirits. The next day I immediately started feeling better.

After I recovered from the pneumonia, I realized I wanted to do more in the animal and humane education world and began writing books about animal rescue. Today, I work from home by design, and I get to be with my dogs all day. From time to time, I think about spending an afternoon working in a coffee shop, but I usually end up staying home with my dogs.

I take breaks and play with them, or we go for walks. I find it comforting with them. It happens infrequently, but from time to time when both of them are out of the house, it is eerily quiet. I love walking past them and rubbing an ear or a belly, even just for a moment. The science is right – petting an animal does calm us down.

Speaking of science, I attended a conference in 2014 where I learned about some of the incredible scientific research showing the therapeutic benefits of human connection with animals. When I came home from the conference, I was excitedly sharing what I had learned with a colleague. She suggested I make a documentary film, and I decided to go for it! Since then, I've been learning more and more about the different ways animals can help people therapeutically, including therapy animals, service dogs, and pets.

It dawned on me a couple of years ago that my life has been profoundly affected by animals. Each individual experience didn't have a major impression on me at the time, but in retrospect, it was profound. I have been an active participant in the human-animal bond all along. When I began learning about the research that proved what many of us already know about the power of the human-animal bond, I took note. This is all culminating in my life's work making films that spread awareness of the power of the human-animal bond. The films will enable more people to have access to therapy animals, service dogs, equine therapy, and pets, as well as raise our level of respect for animals all around the world.

Sometimes it's not one life-changing story, but it's a series of smaller stories that aren't quite as obvious. But when you look back, you realize they were guiding you toward something you never would have or could have considered on your own.

The Unicorn Search

Beth Lauren Parrish

My mouth dropped open. I stared at my phone and turned my head to the side. I couldn't believe what I was seeing. I swiped through the photos, read the description, and felt my stomach do flips. Could he be the one? Then I looked at his asking price. I was nervous about telling my husband. The pony was over the budget we discussed.

I began searching for my dream pony, the mystical unicorn that would no doubt have a large helping of experience, a full cup of personality, and a dash of willingness to continue expanding his athleticism as my new potential dance partner. A "fun and safe little gelding" was my mantra. This was extremely important for me, to have a confidence builder.

Even though I had been riding for over 32 years, my last six years were full of trauma. It began when I lost my heart horse, Biffy. He was my prince of an Arabian who was my most precious friend for 13 years. I was numb for a good six months after his passing. A year later, our home was lost to a fire. I was teaching my students on this property, where our horses roamed in the woods on 10 beautiful acres. The animals were all saved, thank goodness, but we were displaced and out of sorts for quite some time. Soon after, I became anemic and found that fibroids in my uterus had grown larger. It was time to send those parts away. I had surgery and began to build up my endurance for riding again. I was teaching and training consistently out of two different barns, but then suffered another loss. My other heart horse, Keeper, was aging rapidly, and he told me it was his time to cross over. He had taken impeccable care of me for my first cross-country event, as well as proved to be a most generous teacher.

A few months later, I fell off Indy, my sweet and sensitive thoroughbred, and tore the ligaments in my knee. Surgery happened for that, including an anchor and screws in the knee. Then, six months later, I slipped on a dog bone on our slick tile floor and broke my femur on the same leg as the knee that was still recovering. I wish I was kidding. That accident led to a nine-inch plate in my leg. And finally, the next year, after going from a wheelchair to a walker, to a cane, to slowly walking with a limp, I woke up one night with severe internal pain. That brought me to take a CT scan, where they discovered my stomach was in my chest, so I had to have surgery for a hiatal hernia.

After the fire, losing two heart horses, and then four surgeries, I was determined to have fun again. With all the agony of recovering and countless hours of physical therapy, I kept seeing myself riding in our arena, with joy and ease. I knew I had to find a very special kind of pony, since I now had all sorts of bionic parts (and I'm only five feet tall). I was on the hunt for a steady, small unicorn who would be into doing what I loved: lower-level dressage and small jumps.

Enter Pepper. Pepper is a Pony of the Americas and has the most gorgeous display of chestnut spots all over his white body. As a bonus feature, he also has the most luxurious naturally wavy tail, comparable to a fancy Andalusian. He really looks like a unicorn! But pretty is as pretty does. I needed to know more. His online ad said he was 13.1 hands, had been a lesson pony, and could do jumping, dressage, driving, trail rides, and even cross country. When I chatted with his seller over the phone, she described how steady he was on the trails, and I knew I had to go meet him.

My husband agreed, and when we arrived, a tiny child was riding him around, going over some small cross-rails. She looked like she didn't want to hop down. I couldn't blame her! This pony was darling and looked like a blast to ride. He was brought to the mounting block so I could hop right on. I started to go up the steps and then stopped. I turned to them and said, "I would like to just walk around with him first in hand. I'd like to get to know his energy and have him get to know me as well."

Pepper then proceeded to sniff my belly, as if taking in and assessing my essence. I walked around and told him I was very happy to meet him and would love to ride him and see if we were a good match. After our walk around the arena, I took a deep breath, sent him love and appreciation, and quietly got on his back.

We moved around, and it took me a couple of laps around the arena to feel completely comfortable with his small frame. He was like riding a large Swiss ball and any little movement I made shifted him. After a few more minutes, we started to get in the groove. He offered me a lovely stretching trot after our canters. We even went over the small jump together twice. I told the seller, after the fact, that I hadn't jumped in several years. I knew he was perfect for me. My husband saw the look in my eyes and then asked the seller if she was willing to negotiate his price. To our delight, she worked it out with us. She even told us that there were a couple of other interested buyers, but she liked that I was an adult who wouldn't outgrow him. She also said she liked the way I rode him, which I thought was a very kind compliment.

My unicorn search was over, and I was over the moon. The night before we went to pick him up to bring him home, I tuned in with his heart and let him know what was going to happen. He told me that he was aware of the move, that my two heart horses, Biffy and Keeper, actually came to him and told him I was going to be his new person. I cried immediately. It was as if they were giving me their blessing.

Now, Pepper and I enjoy dancing in our dressage court, with the tiniest jumps to play with. He keeps me laughing every day and even has worked out how to do the best selfies ever. He has truly given me a "fairy-tail" ending and beginning.

I hope you find a unicorn in your life one day. And, as I always say to end my stories: May the horse be with you. Always.

Healing Beauty

Ginny Jablonski

In late 2019, while I was working in northwest Colorado, I was lucky enough to be invited to visit an equine therapy ranch with a friend near Grand Junction. I had been immersed in the energies of formerly wild mustangs all week, and it was truly a magical experience. During that time, I communicated with more than a dozen mustangs. One by one they shared with me their unhealed wounds, pain, hopes, and visions for the future. They each possessed unique abilities, but most of them were not yet ready to express their gifts.

As is the case with most formerly wild horses I have worked with, they each expressed the need for time and support to heal their past traumas. I learned so much from my interactions from each of them, and the messages they brought forth were helpful in validating that horses are just as unique as humans when it comes to personality, trauma, and life purpose.

The energy in that part of the country is palpable and invigorating. At moments it felt like time had stopped and I was part of the mountain range, yet uplifted by the strong winds that always accompany that part of the country.

We arrived at the ranch in the early morning. The facility sat on a mesa with seemingly endless views of a colorful mesmerizing landscape.

The owner of the ranch was genuine, kind, and welcoming. It was obvious she had been dedicated to this work for a very long time. Her love of horses shone like a radiant light all around her, and the horses responded to her accordingly. She had the energy of a horse whisperer. It was obvious to me that she was, as some would say, the keeper of the herd. As I am writing this paragraph and thinking of her, I clearly see a wild herd of horses stampeding behind her, kicking up dust and bringing a message of oneness and harmony.

I quickly realized almost all of the horses there had been gathered off the range in Colorado, and I was anxious to be able to communicate with them. We spoke with a few of the horses toward the back of the property and eventually made our way to the barn, corrals, and round pens. We were surrounded by horses, and it felt as if we were all experiencing a collective healing that day, both horse and human.

As we approached a small pasture with five horses in it, the owner invited me to speak with any who wished to be heard that day. One by one the horses came forward expressing their unique skills, preferred working environment, and personalities, and several of them had a few interesting questions. In fact, one of the geldings said he really liked working with young girls, but not just any young girls, the ones with long blonde hair in a single French braid. The owner shared that the vision the horse had revealed to me was of the owner's own granddaughter! And, as it turns out, when the granddaughter visits, she always braids her long blonde hair in a single French braid.

One of the last horses to share that day was a gelding. He kept using the word "book," and he spoke of a ministry. He said he very much wanted the owner's husband to finish writing a book. I asked her if her husband was writing a book, and if it had something to do with a ministry. She revealed that he was, in fact, writing a book, but that it was temporarily on hold due to other commitments. She also shared that her husband was indeed a minister! The gelding was adamant that her husband really needed to finish writing his book and that he (the horse) wanted to help him do it. He shared that the reason the book needed to be finished right away was because his herd had plans for him to start writing another book. In fact, he stated it would be a series of three "little books." He shared topics that each of the little books would address, how they would impact people's lives, and even shared what the artwork would look like. The detail he shared was remarkable in every way. He even outlined how the layout of the ranch in the drawings for book would differ from their actual ranch and what the purpose was for each alteration.

Finally, he showed me a vision of the inside of the back cover of the book. It was a watercolor drawing of very tall, almost sheer, red and golden rock cliffs. Below the image there was a paragraph written that I could not quite make out. It felt as if the paragraph described the unknown, to me at least, importance of the cliffs. I described the drawing in the vision I was shown, and the owner exclaimed, "Ginny, these horses were gathered from the Little Book Cliffs here in Colorado!"

I'm pretty sure we both cried at that point. That was the first time I had ever heard of the Little Book Cliffs, or the wild herd of mustangs that lives there.

Roughly eight months later, after losing three recently adopted horses in the first six months of 2020 and one in 2019, my husband and I were sure we would never adopt another horse again. We were devastated by the profound loss we had experienced over the years, especially after we had invested so much of our heart and soul with them. We had loved them for 12 years, 1.5 years, eight months, and eight weeks, respectively, in order of their passing.

To my surprise, in the first week of July, my husband told me he thought it was wrong for us not to have horses on our property and suggested that we begin searching for horses to grow our herd again.

Within days of our conversation, I began to have dreams about Colorado's Little Book Cliffs and the wild mustangs there. I would hear, "Little Book Cliffs, Little Book Cliffs," over and over in my sleep. After two nights of this, I was convinced that at least one of our new horses was going to be from the Little Book Cliffs herd.

From what I knew about the herd, they were only gathered every 10 years and one had taken place not long before. I sent a few messages off to friends in Colorado, and within days, someone suggested I inquire about a mare near Grand Junction.

I waited for a day or so to make the call. I wanted to be certain that we were ready to open our hearts to another potentially devastating loss again, but after making the call it was clear she would be ours! She was 15 years old and was gathered off the range two years prior.

She was bolting under saddle and not safe for the current owner. I was thrilled to hear this – not that she was bolting, of course, but that she was going to be ours!

I soon realized I had no idea what she looked like – I hadn't even asked. I only knew her name was Beauty. So, I asked her owner to send a photograph of her and for permission to communicate with her to make sure she wanted to come and live with us.

That night before I went to sleep, I reached out to her with a message of welcome and love. I said, "I know you are going to live with me, and I don't even know what you look like."

I immediately heard a reply. "Black, black, black," and then, "Black Beauty."

I asked her if she knew who I was and if she wanted to come live with me. I can honestly say she was not convinced she wanted to live with anyone in domestication. She seemed confused and, frankly, very angry. I was not a bit surprised by this.

One of my abilities, in addition to animal communication, is that I can see and sense trauma and unresolved energies in the bodies of both humans and animals. Sadly, Beauty's energy field revealed she was carrying a lot of trauma and energetic wounds. Happily, working with traumatized horses is my passion. It seemed to me that she was going to be just where she needed to be to heal, and with us she would have the ability to do it on her own terms.

She wanted to know why she was taken in the first place. I shared with her my then understanding of the Wild Horse and Burro Program managed by the Bureau of Land Management. I talked about humans, our nature, our flaws, and I apologized for the circumstances that she and her herd found themselves in. Both those who remain, wondering where the others were taken, and those who had been rounded up and adopted into numerous homes.

I also explained that there was no option for her to ever be returned to her herd and that a lifetime home with us may just be the best option for her. She needed someone who would understand her, offer her patience, and have absolutely no expectations during her healing process. I opened my heart to her and asked if she would be willing to feel into the work I do with traumatized horses.

After that exchange, I thanked her for reaching out to me in a dream and revealing herself. I told her I thought it was a sign of great spiritual ability and asked if she was still willing to come live with us. Not only did she say yes, but it was then that she revealed to me that her herd, on a spiritual level, had asked her to come live with us. She explained she was "chosen" by her herd to experience my work and to be a bridge for me to continue my work with them.

When I woke up the next morning there was an email in my in-box with several photographs of a gorgeous black mare named Beauty from the Little Book Cliffs!

We had been told that she got along very well with other horses, but when she arrived, she had great difficulty getting along with our two older rescue mares who were quite fragile. Every time we attempted to introduce them, she was aggressive toward them, and she favored our healthier donkeys.

She was also acting out, squealing and rearing from time to time. She was finally free to express her frustration, and we agreed to give her the space and time she needed to begin to trust us.

I worked with her over the course of several months until one day, she said, "I am beautiful and powerful, but I can't use my power to control others."

From that day forward she was never unkind to another animal on our property. And she went on to say that she wasn't quite ready to have a close relationship with me yet in the physical realm.

Here's a little backstory: When she first came to live with us, she called me out into the pasture and demanded that she wanted to have a friendship with me that was like the one I had with my former heart horse, Blue, who had recently passed away. When I explained that my relationship with Blue took a whole decade to cultivate, she angrily walked away, stating she did not want to wait that long.

After that conversation, her wounds turned into shields. She certainly has her own ideas about things, what some people would describe as control issues. We do spend time together physically, but she is slow to trust that unconditional love is real. She braces against it as if she is surrounded by a wall. As we all know, self-protection from all things good is a symptom of trauma.

My husband does most of Beauty's handling, i.e.: farrier, vet, fly mask, etc. Even though she had consented to those interactions with her previous owner, the circumstances were far different. She was constantly enclosed in a much smaller stall, and training aids were used. When she arrived here, she had freedom in a three-acre pasture, freedom to express herself, and freedom to make choices. It took my husband nearly six months to achieve each of those interactions with her, which demonstrates his incredible patience and dedication to her, as well as his Vaquero training. Her previous owner shared that she had always done better with men than women, and she continued expressing that trait with us.

One day she shared how she really felt with me, and it revealed the extent of her internal struggles. She said, "I'm so afraid of myself, my power, my rage." It was devastating to hear, but I knew we could overcome it together.

Beauty recently asked me to write a book about her extensive healing journey with us. She wants people to know how traumatized wild mustangs can be after being gathered and unceremoniously placed into domestication without their consent. Beauty has asked me to document my work with her and some of my other experiences with animals overcoming trauma. I look forward to sharing her story very soon in an upcoming book titled, "Healing Beauty."

Healing Action Steps

1. If you have little experience with animals, are you open to getting to know them? Or maybe you are a "dog person" or a "cat person" who might actually be a "pets-of-all-kinds" person? Ask yourself what's stopping you from being open to all kinds of animals. Release any negative energy or preconceived thoughts about a certain kind of animal and open yourself to healing that block. Try these ideas to get started at your comfort level:

- Visit a pet shelter to volunteer for dog walking or playing with the kitties.
- Head up a drive to collect food, toys, blankets, heaters, and/or fans to take to your local shelter.
- Talk to friends and family about their experiences and adventures with pets.
- Check out books on the pet you may be interested in from your local library.

2. Are you experiencing a difficult situation? Step out of your situation for a moment by tapping into the unconditional love of animals. Cuddle with a purring cat, therapeutically pet and brush a horse, throw a ball with a dog, or watch fish swim around in their zen underwater world. Or, simply step outside and listen to the birds chirping or watch the squirrels playing. You also can consider volunteering at a place that works with people and animals in therapy.

3. If permanent pet placement isn't for you, or if you want to open your home to even more animals, consider volunteering to pet sit or to have play dates for a friend or family member's pet. You get to have all the fun and only some of the responsibility!

Affirmations

I am willing to see things differently.
I welcome the good that is present in the moment.
I see with eyes that unconditionally love.

Journal Prompts

Do you identify with one kind of animal or lots of animals? What do you think draws you to these animals? Is there a specific experience that made you like or dislike animals? Do you have any good or bad experiences with animals that shaped the kind of person you are today?

Think about the unconditional love of animals and the ways you might not extend that unconditional love to yourself. Then, write a healing apology letter to yourself and see if it helps you work through your feelings, release thoughts and emotions that are not serving you, and even find forgiveness.

What pet or animal has made the biggest positive difference in your life? Reflect on how that animal might have healed your emotional wounds.

Connection

"Some people talk to animals. Not many listen though. That's the problem."
~ A.A. Milne, Winnie-the-Pooh

Have you ever watched a show or been to the zoo and wondered, how there can be such an amazing bond between a person and an animal? This is not something that happens overnight. Over time, trust builds, and magic takes place. I first discovered this when my family moved to a farm.

I spent most of my growing years in a city, but when I was a teenager, my mom decided she wanted to become a farmer. This was a culture shock like nothing I had experienced! I laugh now because I really didn't know what I was doing. Overnight, my life went from big buildings and close neighbors to being surrounded by chickens, rabbits, dogs, cats, and horses. I would get up at 5 a.m. to do chores before school, and I was so scared as I took on responsibility for the care of our animals. But every day, I learned more and more. I started developing trust in my horses, and they also grew to trust me. These relationships developed into spiritual bonds that fulfilled me.

These stories of connection with animals speak to our hearts about empathy, relationships, and overcoming adversity. They also showcase how animals encourage us to expand our hearts by caring for the health and well-being of others.

A Friend by My Side

Marla Patrick

I have always had a passion and love for animals, but when it came to domesticated animals, I considered myself a cat person for most of my life. After an aunt's dog attacked me when I was little, I had always been scared of dogs. It was only after I met my husband, and he became a K9 instructor and handler for our local highway patrol, that I discovered dogs were definitely my "thing." Since meeting my husband, we have always had what could be considered a pack of dogs as part of our family. Saint Bernards, Belgian Malinois, German shepherds ... I love them all. My dogs, being big and on a farm, have preferred to spend the majority of their time running around outside. I was okay with this until my daughter left for college, and my house suddenly became empty and quiet.

When my daughter's longtime boyfriend was killed in a car wreck, she adopted a beagle-basset mix named Brody. I absolutely fell in love with his beagle personality, especially after seeing how he helped my daughter heal, and decided to adopt a beagle of my own.

I have always been big on, "Adopt, don't shop," and a friend suggested an organization called the Beagle Freedom Project. After researching them, I decided that taking in a survivor of laboratory testing – scratch that, laboratory torture – was an endeavor I felt qualified for, considering my husband and I own a boarding, training, and grooming business. I looked through the pictures of dogs available until a particular one jumped out at me. His hunched posture and sad eyes screamed, "I need you."

I immediately applied to adopt Klein. I waited a month but never heard anything. I reached out, and they told me there were 13 families ahead of me wanting to adopt him. So, I decided to look locally for one to adopt.

I came across an 11-week-old female beagle that had two failed surgeries, and because she needed a third, people weren't exactly lining up to adopt her. She was so tiny, and the moment I picked her up, she crawled up into my hair and nuzzled me. She then let out this big, contented sigh, and I knew I had to have her. Without even thinking about it, I looked at the woman and told her I would take her. I named her Tora Inu. My husband, all these years later, still doesn't know how much I paid to adopt her. He knows better than to ask! I would do it all over again, though. In that moment, I found my once-in-a-lifetime dog. I love all my dogs, but this girl is truly my soul dog.

Two weeks later, the Beagle Freedom Project called me and said all the potential homes for Klein had fallen through, as they either couldn't handle his physical issues, or they couldn't handle his emotional issues. I immediately called my husband, and his reply was simply, "So when are we going to get him?"

The day Klein was dropped off, Tora Inu immediately grabbed his leash and began pulling him around the farm. I had never seen anything like it, and to this day, I still haven't. It was like she knew he needed direction, and they have been inseparable since. They are unbelievably bonded.

I had no idea how Klein would change my life. For the first three days, he sat in a corner of my dining room and growled at anyone who got too close to him, except Tora. She would simply lie by him, as if to say, "Hey! You are going to be okay." His physical damage was extensive: his third eyelids and anus are dyed red; he has kidney, spleen, and liver damage; blistering all throughout his intestines; and grand mal seizures. Since they told me stress could induce seizures, I let him be, hoping he would eventually see I was not a threat. On the fourth day, he stopped growling at me. At some point, he decided I was his person, and then proceeded to follow me everywhere. I wasn't allowed to touch him, but he had to know where I was at literally every second of the day.

As time went on, Klein would allow me to touch him about every other time I tried, but only briefly. We also went through months of him startling at the smallest things. We even changed how we walked from our bedroom to the kitchen if he was laying on the couch in the living room (the place where he felt safest), because otherwise he would panic and bolt. I have gouges in my living room floor as reminders of that time. We discovered he hates hats, hoodies, and men in general. Hats and hoodies are now banned from my house. I refused to give up my husband, even for Klein, so we had to make a lot of lifestyle changes to help Klein and my husband co-exist. Luckily, my husband is awesome and did what needed to be done.

We have now had Klein almost eight years, and what most people would find completely odd to do for a dog has become part of our normal routine. We don't wear hoodies or hats around him. We announce ourselves before going into a room he is in if he is sleeping. Klein now sleeps with me and Tora. As I usually go to bed first with the dogs in tow, my husband knows that when he gets in bed, he can't make eye contact with Klein, or he will freak out and bolt. My husband doesn't hug me, kiss me, or even lean over me to look at something I am looking at if Klein is around to see, because it upsets him. Most people probably think we are absolutely insane to make so many concessions for a dog. To that I say, this is a dog that was born in a laboratory and spent the first two and a half years of his life having unspeakable things done to him. He deserves to be happy. If being viewed as a little crazy is what it takes for Klein's happiness, call me crazy all you want.

Klein has come so far and is a far cry from the growling, trembling mess he was when he came to live with us. Tora gets a lot of credit for that, as she refused to allow him to be anything but a normal dog. We joke in our house that Tora bullied Klein into normalcy.

On a serious note, though, Klein is proof that our spirits are more resilient than we give them credit for. Although Klein has his quirks, day to day he is a happy, affectionate, and extremely intelligent dog. The trust he now has in me is humbling. Klein firmly believes that he must be with me at all times (including in the bathroom). I'm okay with that, as I can't imagine life without him. As a result, he goes everywhere with me. Even if he can't go into where I'm going, he is happier waiting for me in our truck than he is at home. Left at home, he panics and attempts to dismantle my house piece by piece. In the truck, he is usually content to just wait for me to come back. I say usually, as I discovered a year or so ago, that he was figuring out the truck a little too well and using it to express what he wants.

The first time I discovered this was when I drove into town to have a meal with my mother-in-law. I loaded up Klein and Tora as it was a nice day, knowing they would be content waiting in the truck. Klein knows he is supposed to stay in the backseat, but he never does. The minute I got out of the truck, he jumped in the front seat and hung out while he waited for me. There was nothing unusual about that. What was unusual was that as I was getting ready to leave about an hour later, we heard the truck horn start honking nonstop. Just one long honnkk. I ran to the window and looked out, and while Tora sat a little too innocently in the front passenger seat, Klein was standing in the driver's seat pressing the horn with his front paws, grinning ear to ear and tail wagging. I ran out to the truck and told him to stop. He did … momentarily. The minute I started to walk back in to finish my goodbyes, he started doing it again. It gave everyone a good laugh, but I was a wee bit concerned he had figured out how to summon me to the truck.

Another time I realized he was figuring out the workings of the truck a little too well was on a day I needed to go to the bank. I loaded up Klein and Tora, and off to the bank we went, with my usual routine of going through the drive-through. Both dogs love trips to the bank, as they know the bank has treats for them.

Usually, if it's a day I'm okay with them getting a treat, I roll down the back window, they stand up on their hind legs and stick their heads out, and the teller sends bones for them. On that particular day, I decided they didn't need any, as they were packing on some winter weight, so I didn't roll down the window. I conducted my business, got ready to drive off, and then heard a chuff followed by the teller saying, "You need a couple bones?" I turned around to look at Klein and Tora, trying to figure out how she saw them through the tinted back windows, only to discover that Klein had taken matters into his own paws. He had rolled the window down by himself, then gritched at the teller for his treat. Tora, of course, did not waste the opportunity, and stuck her head out the window, too, while wearing her best sad face.

Needless to say, they both got treats that day, and I have to comfort myself when I leave the truck that it's impossible for Klein to drive off because I have the keys!

I'm so thankful I was able to discover that I am, in fact, a dog person. My life is so much richer because of it. Klein and Tora make me laugh every single day. But more importantly, they remind me that we can endure some pretty horrible stuff and come out okay, as long as we have a friend by our side.

My First Best Friend

Deb Matlock

My first best friend on this amazing earth was a dog named Jenny. Jenny was a beautiful collie adopted by my parents when I was a baby. As the runt of her litter, her future looked a bit bleak. After all, it was the 1970's and the dog rescue movement was not what it is today. Luckily for us, though, a colleague of my father's asked him if he wanted her, and she became a deeply loved member of our family for many years.

When I think of my early childhood, I see Jenny in every memory. She was there for holidays, birthdays, and camping trips. She was also there on regular days, just hanging out on the back porch with us, watching TV, or working in the garden. She was truly a part of the family and was involved in everything where she could be included. I am not sure I realized that she was a different species than me until I was much older. She was not a dog, and I was not a human. We were just friends, attached at the hip.

Jenny was more like a guardian angel to me than anything else. She followed me around, kept me in the yard, and stayed with me in bed at night until I fell asleep. She would bark whenever I was about to do something dangerous like go into the street, and my parents would come running. I suspect they viewed her a bit as a live-in babysitter! Even as a puppy, she was clearly the wiser and more mature of the two of us, and she was a steadfast presence in my life.

Together, she and I navigated the world. We learned to climb the stairs at the same time with both of us struggling as I was only crawling, and she was just a bit too small to easily navigate the steps. We shared toys, naps, and snacks when my mother was not looking. For a precious time, our two different worlds, human and dog, were not that different at all.

My parents were diligent to ensure I respected her, did not sit on her, or pull her hair. I was not allowed to chase her, scare her, or do any number of things we often see in "cute" photos of kids and dogs all over the internet ... photos where the dog is clearly stressed and the adults taking the pictures are clearly oblivious. Instead, my parents helped me see her as an equal and respect her as a fellow being. She was not my dog. We belonged to each other.

When I was 11 years old, the day came that any dog owner profoundly dreads. She had aged, and her hips were no longer working for her. She was not feeling well and was becoming increasingly disoriented. The time had come for her to move into spirit, leaving me without her for the first time in my life. I was devastated, lost, confused, and truly without my anchor. It took me a while to process her death and allow her friendship to become a cherished part of my past, and not a daily reality. Eventually, I moved on, and my precious Jenny became a beloved memory.

Fast forward a decade, and I was a young college dance major standing in the wings for a performance with a notable guest solo artist. I was right behind this incredible dancer as we were waiting for our cue to go onstage, and my nerves were getting the best of me. I was petrified I would make a mistake and ruin this performance. Rumor had it this particular guest solo artist was none too kind when someone messed up his choreography! I was feeling sick to my stomach, paralyzed with fear, and fighting back tears.

All the sudden, from seemingly out of nowhere, I felt Jenny's presence so strongly, it was as if she was standing next to me in physical form. I recall that I even turned around expecting to see her it felt so automatically familiar to have her nearby. She came with such a comforting energy and seemed to relay the message that I should have faith in myself and just go out onstage and have fun. I felt her energy as if she were lying in bed with me like she used to, waiting for me to drift off to sleep. I was stunned and overcome with elation to feel her presence and be reminded of her existence. I was able to collect my-self and perform. It was as if sensing her presence helped remind me that my earthly stresses and dramas of the moment were much smaller than they felt at the time.

This experience shocked me to my core. I had not thought about Jenny in years and was certainly not thinking about her as I was angst-ridden waiting to perform. But she stepped into my life at a time I needed her the most as if to remind me that, together, we grew up and discovered the world. We learned to climb stairs and play on the swings. We learned to wait out rainstorms and snuggle on the couch. As a team, we were unstoppable. Together, still, even with her in spirit, we could go on and face the future, move beyond fear, and step into possibility.

Thank you, Jenny. You will always have my heart. I am indeed who I am today because of you.

For the Children

Lorie Murphey

When I was about four years old, I had an absolute love for animals, and at times it got me in to trouble. I lived on a farm and had lots of outside adventures with chickens, pigs, and horses – some of the best friends I ever had. My first memory of wanting a pet was wanting a bird. I love finches and was determined to have one of my own.

One day, I was determined to catch a finch for a pet. I had a great plan: I propped up a box with a stick, tied a string to it, and put breadcrumbs under the box. The idea was to pull the string when the bird went in for the breadcrumbs. I spent many long days waiting for a bird to take the bait. Needless to say, it never happened! I got in a bit of trouble for using an entire loaf of bread, but I sure had fun trying.

When I was 10, we moved from our farm to a big city. This was a very big change to accept. The love I had for animals was still so strong, but after the move we didn't have any. My mom was the best mom ever and eventually got me a finch. We named him Henry, after Henry Fonda, one of my moms' favorite actors. Well, Henry turned out to be a girl so then we named her Henrietta.

My parents knew I missed the country life very much and all the animals that came with it, especially the horses. All of my siblings (I'm number eight of nine) loved city life, but I still longed for the freedom and peace that horses brought me.

When I was 11, my parents got me a horse for Christmas, and I was so excited! Her name was Lady Luck, and she was white with a light, flea-bitten touch (small specks of black). We were best friends from the moment we met, and I loved her so much.

My agreement with my parents was I had to pay her board at the ranch where she would be staying. I got a job there cleaning 32 stalls a day, six days a week for $60 a month. We were all taught to work hard growing up, and it sure came in handy for what God guided me to do. During that time, I learned how to work and care for horses on a completely different level.

I also started helping at the ranch's summer camps when I was about 14. There were lots of kids that attended those camps and horse lessons, and rumors started going around about the ranch owner abusing some of the long-time students. I was very sheltered growing up, and I had a bit of a hard time understanding it. But things began to change around the ranch, and when I started listening and asking questions, I realized what was going on and was devastated. I had never been approached, and I believe to this day it was because my dad was not one to cross, especially when it came to his kids. My dad stood about 6'1" and was as mean as they came. He's 100 percent American Indian and didn't take any nonsense from anyone. He's a frail gentleman now but still protects his kids as if he were a strapping, young man.

One morning, I got to the ranch for work and was told there had been a theft of some horses. Mine was one of them. My Lady Luck was gone, and everything in my tack room was taken with her. The saddle I had earned, all the grooming items my parents had given me for birthdays, Christmas, etc. Even my boots! I was beyond lost, and that would be the last time I rode for many years. I figured I had worked so hard for what I had and had literally lost my best friend, so what was the point?

But my love of horses never faded, and anytime I saw a horse out and about, it was like I had never seen one before. My heart would melt with both excitement and pain.

As I grew up and finished school and started my career, I thought about horses a little less and didn't talk much about them. But after I married and had an amazing baby girl, something came over me. I knew I wanted to give her the best life ever, and what better way to do that than getting her on a horse!

We ended up with three horses relatively quickly. Horses were a missing piece of me that nothing else could fill, and right away I found my way back to the peace I had missed for so long. Now, I can't imagine another moment of my life without the companionship of my horses and other furry family members.

God has always played a major role in all I do, and he put it on my heart a few years after we adopted the three horses to purchase a ranch. I ultimately learned more about what happened at the ranch where I worked, and it sickened me. I even found out later that the ranch owner had sold Lady Luck!

I wanted my ranch to be dedicated to being a safe, fun, stress-free place for kids, a place they can simply be kids. Thankfully, my ranch became a huge success, with over 2,500 kids coming through each year.

I run the ranch by myself (with the help of my sweet daughter during summer camp season,) but it's usually me tending to everything. I'm so very proud of my accomplishment and dedication to making sure each kiddo who comes through feels safe and carefree. I've gotten many of them hooked on horses, too!

I've now dedicated my life to helping kids and creating a safe place to be at peace. Two of the most precious things God has given me are my daughter and a love of horses. Today, my ranch is a place to share that love and to heal children with the help of horses.

"But whoso shall offend one of these little ones which believe in me, it were better for him that a millstone were hanged about his neck, and that he were drowned in the depth of the sea." (Matthew 18:6)

A Horse, a Boy, and Undying Love

Naomi McDonald

Contemplation is the highest form of activity. The very act of reflecting on an idea sets the process of creation into action. - Aristotle

Wouldn't it be wonderful if a stolen horse could tell us he had ridden in a trailer for four hours and gotten out at 17th Street North? Many hours of heartache could be resolved if our lost beagle could tell us she was in a culvert under the Riverside bridge, across the street from Quick Trip.

Instead, I receive images of houses, fences, cars, and bodies of water that could be anywhere in an animal's consciousness. Meaning, it can be hard to differentiate between past and present, near and far. Yet, here's a story that shows how the power of reflection, intention, love, and prayer can have a profound and positive impact on our lives:

"My son's horse was stolen over a year ago," Shirley said. "Mark is 14 and still cries at night. It breaks my heart." Shirley was silent for a few seconds as if gathering up her nerve. "My chiropractor said his wife heard from a friend in Wichita that her sister lost a cat and you helped her find it."

I'm often referred through a several-person grapevine. In Shirley's case, desperation drove her to make the call. Shirley emailed a photo of a lovely, fit, sorrel gelding with four white socks and a white blaze down his face — Buster.

I felt Buster's presence in seconds.

Me: Buster, can you describe your surroundings?

Buster: Chain link fence, large tree, red truck. I'm afraid.

Me: I felt Buster tremble. In the image I received, he was bone thin. Old shoes on his feet caused his hoofs to be so long he stumbled. I saw a large, bearded man in dirty coveralls.

Me: Why are you afraid?

Buster: All the horses are crowded together bumping me. My legs and feet hurt. People are shouting all around.

"It sounds like he's going or has gone through the Bristol sale," I told Shirley. "I feel his fear."

"I would know it if he was there," the woman said. "I've taken flyers and photos to the authorities multiple times. Heck, I've pasted this town and surrounding towns with flyers. If Buster steps a foot on the Bristol sale property, someone will call me."

When I thought of this precious gelding at the sale barn, I trembled, and my throat constricted. His fear had felt so real. I knew many of the horses sold at the sale were packed like sardines into large vans and taken to slaughter. Shirley had done her homework and exhausted all her resources.

"Buster could be somewhere else or at a sale in another state," I told the woman. "I wish I could be of more help. There is something you and Mark can do. It might be different than anything you've done before, but it's been known to work."

"Anything. I don't care. Anything that might bring my son's horse home."

"Buster is already connected to you and Mark. You can strengthen that connection by imagining your horse in your mind and attaching a golden chord from your hearts to his. Contemplate or reflect his connection back to you. Feel how wonderful it will be when you see him again. Nudge the universe into action and let the synchronistic events fall into place that can bring him home. Then, give thanks as if it has already happened."

A week later, Shirley called. "We did it!" she said. "Mark and I both kept visualizing the chord. We kept hugging him in our minds. My son kept holding his glove, so he could smell Buster. We kept thanking God for bringing him home."

"And?" I could feel her excitement through the phone line.

"I heard it, or I felt it, or I something'd it." Shirley took in a breath. "I don't know, but suddenly I knew to take Buster's photo back to the Bristol sale."

"Mark approached one of the barn cleaners as he was getting in a red truck. The young man remembered a sorrel horse with four tall white socks going through several months before. He told Mark, 'The horse was skinny and filthy, but those tall socks and that white blaze were unmistakable.'

"A lady bought Buster nine months ago," Shirley exclaimed. "The sale barn had lost my first notice. He had already gone through when I took the second and third."

"Is Buster home now?" I asked.

"Yes! When we drove up to the lady's property with the police, Buster was standing in a chain-link yard with a giant oak tree. He's fat and healthy and shiny. You mixed it all up."

"I did," I said. "I mixed it all up. It's as if I had connected to a database and pulled out the most intense images and feelings without the timeline."

"I feel sorry for the lady," Shirley added. "She bought Buster in good faith, but we have his registration papers. There is no denying he is Mark's horse. The sale officials are apologetic, of course, and they will refund her money. But she loves Buster. Mark has offered to have her come over and ride."

I was thrilled for the family and happy for Buster to be safely home again.

When I first learned of the Golden Chord meditation exercise, I could not see how contemplation could be more powerful than physical action. Speaking telepathically to animals was weird enough, why add something harder to believe into the mix? I could not have been more wrong.

Shirley and Mark accomplished two distinct but interfacing phenomena — or powerful woo-woo, as I once would have called it.

First, by visualizing the chord between their hearts, they strengthened the very fabric of the universe that held them together. As their bond strengthened, the Divine Matrix simply let events fall into place. Shirley knew to go back to the sale barn at the right time to catch the young man with a red truck who remembered Buster ... Absolutely amazing!

Second, Mark's reveling in the scent of his horse, imagining his arms around solid warmth, feeling what it would be like to be reunited with his loved one — this and giving thanks put them in perfect alignment to draw the same vibrational frequency back to them.

Thank you, Buster. The once hard-to-believe philosophies, like that of Aristotle, now feel profoundly and inexplicably right. Because of my experience with you and your family, contemplation and positive prayer is my first line of action. As a result, more of our lost furry family members are finding their way home.

How many other ways can we improve the quality of our lives with reflection, contemplation, and positive thoughts?

Lessons from a Red-Tailed Hawk

Linda Roberts

Have you ever seen and appreciated a red-tailed hawk flying in the sky? Their beauty and vision have always mesmerized me. If you've ever wondered what a red-tailed hawk is thinking, I have an insider's perspective for you as an animal communicator who cared for one for nine years.

Hawk was in captivity at the local forest preserve due to an injury that prohibited her from soaring to the heights needed to survive in the wild and hunt for herself long term. At the preserve, she was trained to become the educational team mascot, and the team would take her to classrooms and on field trips to educate children and adults about the beauty, power, and grace of wild animals.

Hawk had an air about her that was regal and determined. She had a sharp eye, always looking around for potential things to hunt. She enjoyed being the center of attention so she was a great asset in the classroom presentations.

I became familiar with Hawk when I became a volunteer for the forest preserve. Being a former elementary school teacher who was going through some major life challenges with the loss of my mother, trying to leave an abusive marriage with financial hardships, and health issues, I also wanted to continue to be with children in some capacity. Children and animals have always brought me joy, and I was hoping to find that joy by volunteering.

As I became familiar with the presentations for the elementary school children at the forest preserve, my next role was to become familiar with handling Hawk and the resident screech owl. Being a lifelong animal lover, I had experience with many different domesticated animals, but I hadn't had a lot of exposure to wild animals. I was excited about my new responsibilities. It was my job to clean Hawk's living quarters, make sure she had fresh water, and feed her.

To keep Hawk manageable and interacting with humans, the protocol for feeding her was to have her jump/fly on to my thick leather glove while I held a dead rat or mouse in my hand. I then had the pleasure of watching her tear apart said food. I had to be brave, confident, and have a strong stomach to be able to do this particular task! Even though I was in a very difficult time in my life, I was up for it.

My first day learning how to care for Hawk is such a great memory for me. I was guided into her mews (a large birdhouse) by a staff member who was very experienced in handling Hawk, and she showed me how to spray clean the mews, as well as replenish the water and clean up any bits of rat guts that were left behind. As I was shown how to wear the glove and how to cue Hawk to jump on to that glove, I was excited and cautious. It was amazing to be able to feel the power and the strength and the beauty of this wild animal as she sat upon my arm. I took a deep breath and stayed calm even though I was very excited to have her on my arm. The staff member then placed a deceased rat in my hand, and Hawk proceeded to tear the rat apart! Typically, she would decapitate the rat and then pull some of the innards out, shaking them off of her beak and having them fall to the ground. But not this time. As she ate this rat, she deliberately threw rat guts and bloody organs on my coat. I was covered in rat guts, and the smell was putrid. The staff member snickered and laughed out loud. She commented that she had never witnessed Hawk so deliberately make a mess on somebody. I asked Hawk, "Why did I get this special treatment?" She replied, "You're a mess, clean yourself up! Get your act together."

She also said I needed to have an awareness of myself and to clear myself of the things I no longer needed. She thought I was holding onto too many worn-out beliefs and feelings. This had been her initiation to see if I had the "guts" to stick around to care for her. Hawk was establishing herself as a mentor and teacher in my life, and she certainly got my attention with her initiation!

As we enter new periods in our lives, we do have to step into a place of being uncomfortable, in order to make some of those changes that our heart desires. I am honored to have spent nine years of my life taking care of Hawk. During her feedings, she and I always had conversations where she would give me a bit of wisdom to help me through my difficult life experiences. There were days I was sad and distraught about something going on in my life. Each time I went out to visit Hawk, I knew I had to be confident because she would sense my weakness, which could be dangerous to me. This led me to find courage, somewhere deep down within me, with everything in my life. I know she helped me find that courage.

I also was always inspired by Hawk's regal presence. I was drawn to this quality like a magnet, knowing I had to be as regal and confident in myself as she was with her situation.

There were many times she told me how dissatisfied she was being semi-domesticated, as she wanted to soar free. She was always looking to the skies, listening to her fellow hawk tribe floating in the skies above her, as she longed to hunt once again.

There were a few times she was able to hunt for herself. Once, a snake was silly enough to slither into her mews. Or at times, a chipmunk or field mouse would find their way to her area, but not for long, because she had a sharp eye and was eager to hunt and eat any small creature. Even though she couldn't fly, she was adept at hunting, which is a natural instinct for all wild animals.

In one of the conversations Hawk and I had, she compared herself to me. She said, "Look at the container you've put yourself in." And then continued, "Look at the container I have found myself in. Having a broken wing being unable to hunt for myself. These things frustrate me, but I make the most of it and I am not going to let it get me down."

I realized in having this conversation with Hawk that she was more to me than an animal in my care. She was a mentor and a teacher who reminded me to watch my perspective because if we feel trapped, we're going to act differently than if we feel empowered. She showed me she was still empowered in captivity. This was a reminder I needed.

On one summer day, I went out to feed Hawk and, after she ate, she acted strangely and told me she was still hungry. I told her she had eaten her allotted portion and then went about my duties of cleaning her enclosure. I removed the safety leather glove and sprayed down her mews, cleaning away the feathers and residue that had built up inside of her home. She was not a fan of the hose so when I put it down, she charged at me on the ground, spreading her wings, looking like a mini-pterodactyl. I jumped and stepped out of the mews for safety, closing the door behind me and watching her as she confiscated my leather glove. Yep, she sat on top of the leather glove and demanded she get more food. She commented on how embarrassing it would be for me to say I lost the leather glove to her, and this is when I realized she was quite the negotiator!

I returned to the building to find her more food. I did discover one mouse that was ready to be fed to one of the other birds. Making sure the other birds had what they needed, I returned back to Hawk. I placed the mouse on the ground, away from the glove, and she took the mouse in her talons and swallowed it immediately, giving me just enough time to capture my leather glove and exit safely.

Knowing she was teaching me something with that adrenal-pumping experience, I asked her, "Why did you do that?" She proceeded to tell me, when you want something, you need to go for it. You are stalling with certain things in your life. Take action, don't hesitate, seize the day!

During my daily meditation, I reflected on this particular experience with Hawk. I viewed things from her perspective and from my perspective. I realized she was correct, that I had not taken action or created the life I really wanted. She knew I had dreams of a different life, and she felt I was dragging my feet with making it a reality. I'm so deeply grateful to her because I did listen to her and take action to create a life I am truly proud of.

There was a memorial service for our beloved Hawk at the forest preserve recently. I was fortunate to attend with almost 20 others who had cared for her for over 33 years of her being in captivity. Raptors live to be about 12 years in the wild, so this was a significant accomplishment for her. We shared tears and touching stories about our regal, sassy, feathered friend. It's amazing how many lives she touched, not only with those who tended to her care but also schoolchildren, visitors to the welcome center, and so many more. She will forever be in my heart with her words of wisdom.

A Divine Communication

Esta Bernstein

My dreams are vivid, direct communications from the other side. It is probably the only time I am able to receive precise divine guidance because sometimes I can't shut much else off while I am awake. While I sleep, lots of information comes to me that I usually remember with uncanny accuracy. My dreams are not only informational but also prophetic, which can be good or bad depending upon the dream. Reoccurring dreams are a big signal for me to pay attention that something will happen in this 3D realm, and I have avoided mishaps by paying attention to them. Or let's say, they don't leave me alone until I do.

In April 2013, I had a dramatic dream unlike any I had before. It began with me walking through a home I did not recognize. The hallway was in the center of a rectangular house, and as I made my way down, I glanced into multiple adjoining rooms, seeing people I had known who had passed on. They just looked at me, not uttering a word. Once I reached the end of the hallway, I turned back around and came upon a bright yellow kitchen that looked like it was from a mid-century farmhouse. I stood in front of the sink and a window covered with flowered curtains. As I pulled back these curtains, the face of a gray horse appeared in the window, and she began speaking frantically to me. She was talking so fast I couldn't understand a word she was saying, but she was clearly upset. I asked her to slow down and what her name was. Her reply was Lava Lady.

Then, the scene changed into something out of a 1960s-type movie with a retro, swirling backdrop, kind of like what you would see in a James Bond or Austin Powers film. In the middle of this swirling backdrop, I was shown what I thought was a fetal kitten. Suddenly, I was awake. I came to realize later that this was not a fetal kitten, but a foal in a horse's womb.

This was one of the strangest dreams I'd ever had, and it haunted me for weeks. The name Lava Lady was never out of my mind, so I set out to research it to see if she was a real horse. Through my investigation, I found two horses named Lava Lady: one was a racehorse in Florida and the other was a racehorse from the early 20th century. I didn't know which one was asking me for help, but she would not let me rest and continued to try to connect with me.

Although Lava Lady's persistence was unusual, I didn't find it unusual that a racehorse would try to connect. During my youth, my family had racehorses so it's an industry entrenched in my blood. Wanting to be a trainer in my younger days, I moved to California, clinging to that image. But, I learned that it was not meant to be. My horse passion turned from racing to breeding and showing Arabians, though neither of those professions merged into the reality I was hoping for. What I did receive from all these experiences was a deep knowledge of how to care for horses, but I had yet to discover the missing piece I would incorporate into my daily activities running an equine rescue.

I called my friend Lisa Larson, explaining the dream, knowing she was the only person who wouldn't think I was nuts. I asked if she could try to communicate with these horses without any other information than what I had. The message I received was one of my most intense and life-changing moments, and as Lady Lava communicated her words of wisdom and plea for help, I was sent through some type of time warp, transported to where she was and listening to the emotional words pouring from her soul. Much of the conversation actually came from both horses, but the discussion that ensued energetically was from the connection of their souls.

The message began with Lady Lava describing what she saw on a daily basis. There were never-ending, lush green pastures, and she was with many other horses. As she was describing her surroundings, which to us humans would seem like horse heaven, a deep feeling of despair flowed through her words. She said the people were nice, but there was no emotional connection to them. It was almost as if she had known what an emotional connection with a person was, but she no longer had it.

She explained she was a broodmare, and this was not the life she wanted, nor did she want her baby to be a racehorse. As the conversation continued, she began to describe why she contacted me. She said I was her only hope and asked if I might be able to find a place for her and these horses.

She told us this was a time in my spiritual evolution where I was going to bring to light to a wider audience the kinds of lives racehorses have. She said when people look at racehorses, they assume they are well taken care of and have everything they could want. However, in reality, they are nothing more than slaves, and it was time the world awakened to it. She also described her knowledge of the Mayan Calendar and its significance but said we as humans have misinterpreted it. She said the Mayan Calendar event was about the new beginning of our change in consciousness and our global spiritual evolution, with lightworkers being called in to begin the awakening process. The catch was that there would only be a change in consciousness if people were willing to listen and if there were enough people willing to speak.

She had a deep concern for the horse species to survive and thrive. Lava Lady showed us images of horses running wild and free, connecting and interconnecting with all of nature. She then showed us an image of that existence no longer being present in this space-time continuum. I began to cry as her words flowed through Lisa, and I felt deeply humbled and slightly confused when she stated I was contacted because I am a friend of the horse and that I understand horses like no other.

She explained that from the horses' perspective, breeding is removing the beauty and wildness of their true nature. She said it has turned them into machines, to the point where broodmares who have babies cannot or do not want to emotionally connect to their foals because the foals don't know how to be real horses in the true, soul sense of the word. She was afraid that what the heart and soul of a horse is and was would cease to exist later on. She said if I could help her and the other horses with her, then I could help many more. The spiritual aspect to this statement was that if she could find the right home, she had much she could teach.

She said that when horses do not perform to their human's expectations, they get thrown away and then don't even know what to be anymore. They don't know how to reconnect ancestrally. She claimed that rescues, especially racehorse rescues, take care of them well, but they aren't helping them come back into the fold of who and what they really are. According to her, most rescues never quite get there because they don't do what I do. They don't connect with them in the same way, they don't talk to them in the same way, they don't communicate with them in the same way, and they don't feel them.

After being taken aback from this intense conversation, Lisa and I took a minute to regroup so we could align ourselves with how to approach what she was asking me to do. Feeling utterly overwhelmed by the task she had just placed on my soul, I tried my best to not fall into feelings of helplessness. When you get a message that all of horse consciousness is looking at you to make a difference in the lives of horses all over the world, you tend to feel rather small!

Lava Lady explained, "This is the reason why we came to you." She said that so many people don't understand that it's not about humans; it's not about the human way of looking at us. It's about humans understanding horses. It is more difficult for humans to understand horses than it is to understand dogs or cats because they don't live with them.

At the close of our conversation, she acknowledged her gratefulness to me, not just for listening and doing what I am doing, but what I am going to do and for being who I am. She said I had heard this lesson before. "You (Esta) are much more important and powerful in this realm, in the mysterious world of horses, in the ethereal world of horses, than you think you are." She said there is a reckoning coming, and she appreciates that I am one of just a few who has the skills to change the direction of that reckoning.

This was actually hard to write, as my ego felt embarrassed that this horse was giving me kudos I didn't feel I deserved. These were her words, not mine, and I would never think of myself with such importance as she did. But maybe within her words was the answer as to why I needed to incarnate back as a human. The horses were not going to be able to speak for themselves so they needed a representative who spoke both languages to interpret their messages and understandings to humans.

Did she choose me because of my background in the racing industry? Did she connect with the mirror image of me, being lost among the masses with no one to connect with? Was she really telling me that I also needed to connect to source to find myself and my true calling? Maybe it was all of the above.

I came away from this experience with the knowledge I had to incorporate spirituality into the daily aspects of my horse rescue and within my own thoughts and feelings about myself. I needed to stand in my power as a conduit of horse/human soul contracts and be open to receiving love and recognition for the good I am able to do in the world. Embracing this self-image has been the most challenging undertaking I have faced. My conversation with Lava Lady brought up deep-seated feelings of lack and my vision of self-worth, but with her continual support in body and in the spirit realm, I have learned never to doubt the power of love and the Divine.

What It Means to Be a Red Barn Horse

Alexis Braswell

It is no secret that Jessie was my favorite Red Barn Horse. In fact, Jessie was one of my favorite horses ever – and I've been around a lot of horses over the last 30 years. As cliché as it might sound, she was special.

Jessie was the first horse I picked for The Red Barn as leader of the Horse Team. The Red Barn is a non-profit that provides equine assisted services to low-income individuals with disabilities and other special circumstances. I had trained other horses to be therapy horses, but I was either working under the guidance of another trainer or working with one of my personal horses that had joined The Red Barn's herd. A lot was riding on Jessie's training for me personally. Jessie taught me more about prepping and training therapy horses than any horse I'd ever worked with, including my own. She was brilliant. She held me accountable, and she made me think – a lot. She challenged me. She made me smile. She made me better.

Jessie taught me the importance of making a plan. More specifically, Jessie frequently reminded me that the horse training plan is, and always should be, based on the needs of the horse. People frequently ask what made me love Jessie so much. I've thought about that a lot, and while I can't define it 100 percent, I think I can get pretty close.

Jessie's work ethic was unparalleled. No matter how hot the Alabama summers got or how hard she had worked the day before, her ears were always up. She would've happily taught 10 lessons in a row if we'd let her. To this day, I have not met a horse with a better work ethic.

Jessie changed lives, and I loved that every time I had the privilege of working with her, I got to watch her make someone's day better. Jessie loved cuddling students, staff, and volunteers. You could see how someone's eyes would light up when Jessie rested her chin on their shoulder for cuddles.

I think my favorite Jessie connection was the one she had with my student, Reid. Reid rode Jessie for the first time in November 2015. The lesson note from that day reads, "Reid's best lesson ever," which is pretty amazing considering Reid had been riding at The Red Barn since 2011. They hit it off from the beginning.

Reid rode Jessie until she got sick in early 2019. At the time Reid began riding Jessie, his anxiety was high, and the barn was his safe place. Once she got sick, he requested to just spend time relaxing with Jessie. For almost a year, with the approval of his parents, Reid's lessons consisted of him lying on Jessie's back and telling her funny stories. You could literally see the tension leave his body as soon as he was with her.

After about a year, Reid told me he was ready to start steering again. He never looked back. Reid went from lying on Jessie bareback to riding independently at the posting trot. In his last lesson on Jessie during February 2019, Reid was learning to change his diagonal at the posting trot. Jessie gave him confidence that I could never have given him as an instructor. He trusted her, and she trusted him. They were the epitome of a team.

A common misconception of autism is that those on the spectrum lack empathy and the ability to connect with others. Reid loved and cared for Jessie. He worried about her when she got sick. Even when he could no longer ride Jessie, he would ask to take time to "just visit and love on her a little."

When it became apparent that Jessie would need to be put down, my heart broke. Not just due to my own connection with her, but for Reid and all the other people who loved her. We called to let Reid's mom know, and she brought Reid out to say goodbye. What I thought would be an incredibly gut-wrenching day turned out to be one of the most memorable and beautiful experiences from my time at The Red Barn.

Reid's love for Jessie was so apparent. He hugged her and thanked her and led her while she ate some grass. After about an hour, he left. Then, he turned around and said he wanted to pray for Jessie. He prayed the most heartfelt prayer I've heard in my life. Thankfully, someone recorded it.

Here is a transcription of Reid's prayer for Jessie:

"Dear Lord, thank you for the time Jessie got to live down here on Earth. Help her to be brave when she goes to Heaven. Lord, just keep us safe. Help us to help her have a good life in Heaven. Lord, we love you very much. Help everybody be happy, and we love you very much, Lord, and we pray for you in Jesus' name. Amen."

That prayer brought comfort to all of us that day on a level we didn't know was possible. Jessie connected to Reid on a level that can't be explained other than by God. What makes Jessie even more incredible is that there are countless other stories out there of her doing the same thing for so many others. She really was special.

Unfortunately, cancer took Jessie from us too soon. I would have loved more time to learn from her, but I am eternally grateful for the four years I had. She made every day at work better. She constantly reminded me why we do what we do and how life changing a bond with a horse can be. There is not a day that goes by at the barn where I don't use something Jessie taught me. Every therapeutic riding program should be so lucky as to have at least one Jessie.

Farm Girl Memories

Abigail Stimpert

Everyone who has grown upon a farm and lived that life has a thousand stories to tell. My story probably isn't much different, but it is my story. On a farm, animals are an extension of your family. They come in all shapes, sizes, and colors, and I think God put something in our hearts that those shapes and sizes all fit into. Each animal has its own personality, and part of the fun of living on a farm is that we have the opportunity to interact with each of them to better understand their unique personalities.

Ever since I can remember, we have cared for animals. I had a busy childhood, but it seemed like there was always room for one more animal in our lives. I'll never forget the litter of piglets Mom rescued, trying to raise a wild bunny, successfully raising a litter of tiny kittens after their mother died, rescuing an owl caught on a field fence, freeing birds that found their way into the greenhouse, trying to help an injured songbird, studying the design of a turtle passing through the yard, and even rescuing honeybees out of the dog's water bowl. I grew up knowing life is important, no matter whose life it is or how short it was designed to be.

As I grew up, the simplicity of farm life became even more precious to me. Simplicity probably isn't the right word because the miracles that occur on a farm every day are not simple. But simplicity is real in the essence of it being a less complicated way of life, a lonelier, quieter way of life than most people on this earth live. I have come to love the joy of a lonelier, quieter life.

On our farm we live to steward what God has given us and we take the care of the land and animals very seriously. There is always more work to do than there are hours in a day, but it's a satisfying feeling at the end of a long, hot day knowing you've given your best and the animals are all safe, well fed, and happy.

Sometimes the farm is full of drama, and springtime often bursts forth with color and activity. We have bottle fed many "bummer lambs" – lambs whose mothers have rejected them for some reason. "Lazarus" (or "Lazzie" for short) was one bummer lamb that was nearly dead on the cold morning we found him frozen to the dirt where he'd been delivered. With the help of some thawed colostrum, he was revived and became an amazing pet. For the first few weeks, Lazzie lived in the house with us. The laundry room became his bedroom and we tried to put diapers on him while he was running around the house, but they never seemed to hold it all. He loved to jump on the "Lazzie-Boy" recliner for a nap and was very angry when we put him in his room at night. Lazzie didn't know he was a lamb. Sometimes he thought he was a human; sometimes he thought he was a dog. Our German shepherds sort of adopted him as their own, and they would race around the yard chasing each other. Every day he would walk with us to the barn to milk the cows. The shadow of his head and ears looked just like he was wearing a cowboy hat as he proudly walked by our side, as if he was protecting us, much like our dogs did.

Feeding a lamb a bottle is very fun; they often get down on their front knees and their little tail is a constant flurry of wool, swishing with great excitement. Lazzie had a tendency to eat his milk too fast, which would make him cough. With each cough, a little fart would escape, always making everyone in the room laugh and sometimes even fart ourselves, leading to even more hilarity!

It was a sad day when Lazzie had to join the rest of the flock. He stood at the fence bleating and pleading for us to take him back home.

Something I had to learn about farm life as a child was the harsh reality of separation and even death. In my heart, I think Lazzie would still be alive if we hadn't put him with the rest of the sheep. He never fit in, and when the rest of the flock would go to pasture, he would often stay at the barn, alone. Sheep are very social creatures, and it broke my heart to see him by himself. When Dad found him dead one cold Sunday morning, we all mourned his loss together. He's the only sheep who resides in our little animal cemetery alongside other precious dogs and cats.

One of my earliest memories with the cows was at about four years old, when I was determined to help Dad milk Plum, a cow that had never learned not to kick. Dad cautioned me to stay back, but I couldn't resist reaching down to help him. As soon as I did, Plum kicked me, nailing my leg with her hoof and covering me in poop. I ran out of the barn crying, but, honestly, it could have been a lot worse! Dad was quick to comfort me and get me cleaned up. And while I loved being "Daddy's little helper," that experience got me banned from the barn for quite a while!

I'll always cherish the memory of seeing a calf born for the first time, helping pull a lamb, and helping deliver a puppy. Those are necessities on a farm, but it is still a privilege for me. The miracle of life is amazing.

I'll never forget the tiny, lifeless form of a newborn puppy in my hand; that image left an indelible impression on my mind. We had decided to raise a few litters of German shepherd puppies and share the joy of the breed with others. Our dog Guinevere went into labor one morning when I was the only one in the house. She knew what she was doing so I wasn't too worried about her, but we felt it was important that someone be there with her during labor. While I was alone, a little guy was born, but even after Mama removed his sac, he still wasn't breathing. I quickly jumped into action and suctioned his nostrils, rubbed him vigorously, and said a quick prayer: "Jesus, help this little baby live!" Instantly, a little squeak of air came out, and he began to breathe. I felt I had just witnessed a true miracle!

Proverbs 12:10 says, "A righteous man regards the life of his animals." Taking life for granted is pretty easy to do, even on a farm. There are days when everything seems the same, no changes, no disasters, no craziness, and then in an instant, everything changes.

One calm day, we got a call to rush home because our bull had broken his leg. It was a compound fracture, meaning the bone was protruding out of the skin. We called the vet, hoping he would consider trying to repair it in some way, but he didn't feel that was possible. The risk of infection with an open wound and the lack of mobility would surely kill him. He recommended putting him down. Those decisions are decisions no one wants to make, but we have to make them for the overall good. That bull ended up providing us with a freezer full of meat to help meet our physical needs.

There's a lot of prayer that goes into the care of our animals here. We don't just pray for them when they are sick or injured; we pray daily for their well-being and health. As a teenager, my sister and I spent most of a day with an injured cow, praying over her and believing in faith that she would walk again. "The effectual, fervent prayer of a righteous man availeth much" (James 5:16) is a verse that kept coming to mind. That sweet cow did recover and had many more years of happy grazing.

The Bible tells us that each man's days are numbered. We never know what a day will bring, how we'll be changed or grow from the decisions we make, how we'll respond to a difficult call, or where we'll find a new litter of kittens. But we have the reassurance of knowing we're doing what God called us to do: care for the land and the animals He created and blessed us with. Every day I ask myself what I can do to make the life of my animal friends better, to ensure they are safe, well fed, clean, and happy.

When God Says, "Wait."

Hannah Stimpert

"Jesus, please give me a horse. Amen." This short bedtime prayer was the cry of my four-year-old heart. I started praying that prayer every day after a dream of having a horse almost came true ...

"Hannah, wake up! There's a horse in the yard!"

I opened my eyes to a beautiful summer morning, and my sister Abby was yelling at me as she looked out our bedroom window. I didn't believe her; it seemed too good to be true! I was three years old and had waited all my life for this moment – as do most horse-crazy girls!

Once I realized Abby was serious, I scampered to find some quick clothes to put on. I clearly remember thinking, "I'm so unprepared! I can't even find the right clothes to wear."

The memory is as vivid as yesterday: this dark brown animal had a black mane and tail with a white star and white socks. Our family gathered around the surprise guest, wondering where he came from. Mom put me up on his back for a few fleeting moments. I was in love! Life was perfect.

Then ... "Snickers!" A very grumpy looking lady was stomping down our driveway. Apparently, Snickers had too often put his owner's "knickers in a wad," as she told us how he'd been running away recently.

My excitement soared when she offered him to us for $300. But my parents declined, not being able to afford it at the time or having an adequate place to put him. As she led him away, I felt my dream being taken with him. My chance of being a three-year-old cowgirl was walking away from me. We never saw Snickers again, but my daily bedtime prayer always consisted of the horse I would someday have.

A few years later, our family got a pair of Haflinger draft horses in the hopes of them pulling our hay wagon. As time moved on, the pair lounged in the pasture without getting the training they needed. As children, we weren't allowed to spend much time with them, but Abby and I constantly daydreamed of our own horse ranches filled with horses that never had to leave us.

In the meantime, I spent my childhood loving on and playing with our very tame, small dairy herd. I loved our dairy cows. I raised each of them with a bottle and a kiss and loved growing up caressing their fuzzy heads and long eyelashes.

I didn't have a horse, but what I did have was a cowgirl hat, a western belt, and a lasso. (The boots came later in life.) Those ornery little calves were somewhat of a substitute for a horse and made me one of the happiest little cowgirls around. Still, I wouldn't have been in want if Snickers had been there, helping raise me through my tomboy years.

The other farm critters played a role in helping raise me, too. My chicken, Princess; Lily the lamb, Abraham, our loving German shepherd; and many others. For my 12th birthday, I asked my grandma for one of her kittens. She was named Mindy. Mindy was a gray tabby with huge, green inquisitive eyes. She was every ounce as intelligent as she looked, except when she finished cleaning herself and forgot to pull her tongue back in! (Her offspring have kept that same goofy tradition.) I fell head-over-heels for Mindy, and I still love her with all my heart. Mindy spent four short years with me and my family. She was a ray of sunshine each day of those years. One of her cutest antics was playing "fetch" with my lip balm. We would often spend an evening laughing together around a warm fire as we played fetch with Mindy. We would throw the small tube down the stairs, and she would run down, retrieve it, and bring it back to us for another go-around. She wanted to participate in every little project we had going on at the farm, from climbing the ladder to helping on the roof, patiently waiting for a drink of warm milk twice a day at the barn, and scratching at my bedroom window to be let inside.

Mindy developed an illness that ended up taking her life. For several days leading up to her death, I nursed her around the clock. I tried to keep her comfortable and slept beside her. Mindy was the first pet that was totally mine and, in some ways, she filled a void for the horse I never had. I didn't want to accept the reality of her inevitable death but after a couple days, I prayed that if she were to die, that she would go quickly. When she passed, I grieved her loss deeply. Now I believe God was preparing me for the loss of other loved ones later in my life. When God puts me through something I don't understand, I've learned to be thankful for each new day and for the memories of those loved ones.

"Weeping may endure for a night, but joy comes in the morning." This verse from Psalm 30 was given to my Mom after a miscarriage and shortly before I was born. I was born at seven in the morning and given the middle name Joy. That verse has always been special to me because as I look back at things like the loss of Mindy and others later on, I can see how God had something else waiting for me. I smile because of the joy of a new season in life or the joy of getting to know a new animal. Every hardship makes us a little stronger if we choose to let it.

Once I was a teenager, I poured over horses for sale online for months. I had earned my own money to spend, but it seemed the ones within my price range never worked out and I was getting discouraged. One Sunday afternoon, I found a gorgeous 15-year-old Paint that caught my eye – and she was within my budget! Could it be true? My teenage heart wasn't going to let this one slide. The day we picked up Honey felt surreal. Oh, my stars, was she beautiful! Her honey-colored coat, her one blue eye and one brown eye, her large white face, her white legs, and her multicolored tail still give me chills when I see her! Abby and I prayed that we, as her new greenhorn owners, would do her justice.

But she came with a few unexpected issues. Just when we thought our prayers were being answered, we realized that we had to work for it – we had to do our part to earn her trust and love. She also had some tenderness and sensitivity that prevented us from riding her right away. We had to keep encouraging ourselves and keep our spirits up as we patiently waited for her to trust us.

Honey has been good for me. I've learned a lot about trust and patience from her. With time and advice from good friends, I am learning that love is everything she needs. A transformation is occurring as we come to understand one another more and more. She's helped me see more of my own imperfections as I attempt to communicate with her. Honey is helping me grow up that giddy, three-year-old horse girl that still lives inside me.

Rewarding positive behavior is such an amazing way to communicate with any animal, and Honey is no exception. She is learning that good behavior is what's expected when we see her, rather than her deciding how our time together is going to be spent. I've started working with her bareback and she's reacting positively. The more I work with her, the more confident I become. I've realized that I have to hold her accountable more (which is holding myself accountable, too) and not just give into her cuteness.

Being able to hug her, brush her, treat her sunburned nose, and see her perk up when she sees me coming is everything I imagined about having my own horse. When you love an animal, they don't take anything from you, they give, give, give – filling areas in your heart you didn't know existed.

I've learned that sometimes what looks like a "No" is God really just saying, "Wait." In His wisdom, He knows what's best for us and allows us to grow out of our comfort zone. Waiting isn't always easy, but we usually have a lot of growing up to do while it's going on. I know Honey was worth the wait! Waiting can help us appreciate not only what we don't have yet but also the other things around us that usually go unnoticed. Joy does come in the morning, and there is always something new to experience and look forward to.

This is where I want to be. These are the boots I want to walk in. This country life is for me; I wouldn't trade it for the world. Every flower I smell, every shooting star I see, I know that I'm home. This is where I'm supposed to be, right here underneath the big Kansas sky. It's not a fairy-tale ending, but I know I'm going to live happily ever after!

Letting Go and Holding On

Donna Palamar

I have an interesting story. I was found in a car with my babies and taken to a kill shelter. Ms. Pat from Ms. Pat's Cats rescued all of us! She took great care of us, inside and out, head to toe. She was able to find good homes for all of my babies, but then it was my turn …

I was perfectly fine living on my own. I worked many hours and really didn't have time to take care of a pet. Besides, there were three wonderful cats for me to take care of at work and I got my cat "fix" there. My friends and family had pets I visited often. Little did I know that things would soon be changing.

It was late that night, and Pat took me over to Petco and put me in a strange cage. I didn't understand what was going on. I was cramped and scared and lonely. I missed my kittens, and this strange place was cold. It was a rough night. I smelled and heard the other animals. Some of them were having a hard time with this situation, too. How do I get out of here?

It was an ordinary day. I had promised to take Samantha, my niece, to Petco. We visited every few months to get treats for her cats and also wandered around to say hello to all the fish, ferrets, and every other creature, making sure all received a "hello." This usually took a while! But, this day, as soon as we walked in, I turned and immediately saw her. She stared at me as I walked to her and looked at me as if to say, "What am I doing here? Get me out! C'mon lady, let's go!" Uh-oh, this was no ordinary encounter – this was a rescue mission! I had to save her.

I made it through the night. Didn't get much sleep. It was nerve-racking knowing there were birds here and I couldn't get them — and dogs, too! I don't particularly like dogs. I prefer to chase after them! Not long ago, I lived on the streets and had to constantly defend myself and my babies. That's how we wound up in the car. That's how my feet were injured, from all the fights. But today ... I saw her! She walked in the store and immediately turned to look in my direction. Our eyes met. I tried to tell her I needed out of this prison. Would she help me? Would she rescue me and be my mom?

She didn't seem like a typical cat and was determined to get out of there. There was no age, gender, or name on the cage so I had no idea who she was, but I knew she had me by the heartstrings. It felt like she had made the decision to go home with me, and I needed to go along with the plan.

But then she left, and I couldn't stop thinking about her. I just knew she was the one! How long would it take her to realize that I'm her one?

When we left I couldn't stop thinking about her. I couldn't leave her there. After many letters to the apartment complex where I lived, (which forbade cats), and other assorted hoop jumping, I was able to bring her home with me! Her cute cat eyes worked like a charm. What a smart cat.

She came back! She's here, she's really here! She's breakin' me out! Wait ... another cage ... a portable one. They keep getting smaller. Where are we going? I wonder what my new home will be like. Oh, my goodness, will there be a dog there? I hope not, I've had enough of those.

I found out her name was April based on the vet's estimation of her birthday. She was about a year and a half old and had been through a lot: living on the streets, being a young mom, having to be on the defense most of the time. I was excited and overwhelmed to take her home, where she could play and hide and explore in safety. I hadn't had a pet in almost a decade. I was way overdue, and April had volunteered for the spot in my heart and in my home.

It's nice here. Lots of hiding places and sunny windows to sit in. Sometimes I see dogs outside. Mostly, I watch the squirrels and birds. They keep me entertained between cat naps. My person, Donna, smiles at me and gives me treats. And I love playing soccer with my ballie! I line the ball up at the top of the stairs, I push the ball, and then I run down the stairs really fast to get to the bottom of the stairs before it does, all while meowing. I usually win. I practice a lot. Maybe I'll be in the Olympics one day.

Sometimes we play fetch. I bring the ball to Donna, and she'll throw it so I can run, grab it, and bring it back to her. I like her more and more. She has boxes and bags for me to play with, too. I like shredding them with my claws and teeth. I pretend they are dogs. Gotta keep my skills up, you never know when a dog can pop up outta nowhere! They do that sort of thing, you know. Sometimes I shred her mail. She doesn't really like that, though. Donna has friends come over, and I love company! Haseena comes to visit from South Africa at least two times a year, and we hang out and spend time together. She calls me her "kitty niece." I look forward to seeing her.

What that cat can do with a box or bag is astounding. Let's not talk about the mail ... there's nothing much left when she's done with it! I think she has talons, not claws. Her feet and claws were visibly injured from before, but she manages well. At first, she wouldn't let me pet her or pick her up. Very independent. Aloof. Unsure. The one thing she liked to do when she started to warm up to me was, of course, walk across my computer keyboard while I was using it! I would type with my right hand and use my left hand to keep her at bay. One day, she stopped pushing back against my hand. I looked over, and her head was resting in my palm and she was fast asleep. She trusted me. She just needed love and affection on her own terms. I understand.

I went in a car to meet Donna's dad, Pete. He likes having me with him and sneaks me all kinds of treats, even the ones Donna said not to. He brushes me and makes all kinds of homemade toys so we can play together. Stanley, Pete's best friend, comes over a lot to bring me treats and toys. I like it here. I always have company. I look out of the window and can almost get those birds! There are tons of squirrels here, too, but Pete chases them away. He likes the ducks that visit, and he feeds them and gives them water. He has hummingbirds he looks after, an occasional fox, a few groundhogs, and chipmunks that torment me by coming really close to the window. They know I can't get them so they stop and stare at me! They do this every day ... some days it's exhausting. And, of course, many dogs walk by. I told you, they always come out of nowhere.

I can hardly keep up with Pete. He goes out for the paper or the lottery at least twice a day. He also goes outside to putter around with the flowers and bird feeders. Pete knows how to take cat naps, too. He's almost better at it that I am. Donna comes to visit to check on us. One day Pete went out and didn't come home. I miss him. He was my buddy. Sometimes I cry.

I had a dilemma. My dad was home all day and was lonely after my stepmom had passed away a few years prior. He was an hour and a half away, and it wasn't easy to visit often. April, too, was home alone during the day and probably lonely as well. I worried about both of them so my solution was to put them together. I thought they could each have constant companionship and would bond and have fun. And that they did.

My dad held a coffee klatch most days. Stanley from next door would come over, and April would go running to greet him. He was, after all, there to visit her! April lived with my dad for a little over a year until he had a heart attack. He was tough and hung on for about a week before finally surrendering. He never came home from the hospital. I miss him tremendously. He was my world. I cry a lot.

Back into the cat carrier I went. Not willingly. I had to be drugged, actually. But I moved back in with Donna at a new place. Truth be told, I haven't exercised in a while so I'm happy it's on the second floor so I can play with my ballie again! Guess what? I have a new one! It's even better. It's lighter, and I get to flip it all around. I also have a collection of paper clips, twisty ties, and some string. I miss Pete a lot. But it sure is good to be with Donna again. I missed her more than I realized. She bought me a cat tree. I get so excited that I run all around and then to the top of the tree. Sometimes I try to climb the ceiling but haven't figured out how to do that yet. Donna says I act like a monkey! That's why she calls me MONK — short for monkey.

Sharing April with my dad was not easy for me. It was like giving up a child, and even though she was in good hands, I missed her constantly. Having her back was bittersweet. I loved having her with me, but it was hard to deal with my father's death. April held space for me when I was sad and knew when I needed her nearby. Now, when I'm feeling silly, we run around chasing each other, and I laugh hysterically. She even has a "safe" spot where she cannot be caught. It's like playing tag. When I get home in the evening, April runs to me, saying hello. I love my Monk! I really missed her.

Lately, Donna's been working from home — and I love it. We cuddle more, play more, and of course snack more! She's almost as good as Pete now with the treats. With lots of practice, she'll be a pro in no time. She's also doing a great job with the naps and the cuddling. I am glad we have each other. I am safe and happy here. It feels so good that I found Donna and my forever home. I love her!

April and I have had a lot of time lately to bond even more. We spent a lot of time snacking – I think she's onto something! We've even perfected synchronized napping. April has been with me through many experiences and adventures, and I tell her I love her every chance I get. How did she know I needed her? How did she know I needed to be loved? How did she know we'd make a great team? She means the world to me. I love having her here. I'm glad she found me.

Gabriel's Story

Sharon Dilley

I first met Gabriel when he was six months old and skinny to the point of malnourishment. He came through the door of my veterinarian's office in need of a forever home. The people at the vet office were aware of my background with training and re-homing dogs for service and knew I was looking for a pup to teach manners and life skills to so the dog could become a new partner for a veteran.

This scraggly, little yellow Lab was so incredibly loving, leaning on my leg the entire time during our first meeting. As I listened to his story, I knew I would be driving home with him in my backseat. He was skin wrapped around the shape of dog bones, yet he loved and reached out to me.

Twenty-four hours after bringing him home, I took him to his first service dog class, which was a group of five-month-old German shepherd pups who had already been attending class for several weeks.

I dropped the leash as I prepared my teaching materials. Before I could grab it to bring him back, he nosed his way past a young German shepherd and climbed into the lap of the dog's handler.

"What did he think he was doing?" I gasped inwardly.

The room grew silent as everyone stopped and watched as this little yellow dog made of skin and bones continued around the entire circle, ignoring all of the canine body language to "stay away" and instead climbed into each veteran's lap. He did not miss a single human in attendance that night.

I held back tears, realizing that no matter where he came from, he had an incredible ability to love and connect with humans, despite the cruel treatment he had endured before coming to live with me. We named him Gabriel that night, because in that moment, we recognized he was more angel than dog. I recognized as well that his trait of gentleness would help him become someone's angel in the future.

But it would be a long path to wholeness.

Gabriel needed time to heal, he needed nutrient-rich food, exercise to strengthen his muscles, and connection with a human he could always depend on before he would have the capacity to help a veteran long-term. My plan for teaching a few service dog behaviors and sending him to a veteran evaporated when I realized the magnitude of damage inflicted upon him in his first six months of life.

I discovered this on our first day together.

I was preparing to take a shower, when I placed Gabriel in a kennel. This is something I do with all of my new charges, when they are going to be left unsupervised for any amount of time, in an effort to protect them and my home from unwanted behavior.

In the middle of my shower, it sounded like the walls were coming down—there was so much commotion coming from the area where I left him. I quickly went to him and found him freaking out and thrashing against the sides and top of the crate so much his nose was already bloody from banging the top of the kennel.

This sweet and tender little dog was in a full-blown anxiety attack because I put him in a kennel, which to a trained dog would be a place of comfort, but to Gabriel was a place of terror.

At this point I started researching where Gabriel came from and discovered he came from a dog auction in Missouri. I learned he had spent his entire life locked up, and to be placed in another kennel made him afraid that he would never get out again.

That was the last time I ever kenneled Gabriel.

But the great gift in this discovery was that it invited me to deepen my practice and awareness of how I help dogs discover who they truly are. Gabriel's true nature was one of sweetness and love – and my job would be to help him remember that place of wholeness.

As a trainer, I understand there are important pieces involved in supporting and encouraging a dog's well-being. I recognize these pieces as 1. Connection 2. Meeting their needs and 3. Providing a safe and nurturing environment.

I immediately started to put these pieces of Gabriel's puzzle together, so not only would he someday have the life skills to be a perfect angel service dog for someone, but he would also be able to connect once again to his own deep well-being.

Meeting Gabriel's needs became my top priority. He needed nutrition, both physically and emotionally. He needed to run and swim to build muscles that had not developed properly, and he needed a safe environment where he could learn how to trust humans. We provided everything for him: healthy and consistent food, long walks, plenty of play time with other dogs, and simple evenings just lying in our laps.

By building a foundation of connection, providing a safe environment, and meeting Gabriel's needs, we automatically engaged with him on a level he had never experienced before, and he began to learn what it felt like to feel good in his mind and body. Over time, Gabriel began to realize he could depend on us, and we built the trust that was lacking. Once that trust was established, he had the peace of mind to learn the life skills necessary to become an amazing service dog.

Dogs are just like humans in this way. When they remember their wholeness, the things they are capable of are limitless. It was my great honor to be a part of this journey with Gabriel, and it continues to be the inspiration that guides me with every dog I work with.

I learn from every dog I encounter. They are such incredible, loving beings. We sell them short and don't even realize their potential to positively impact our lives. Yes, it is more difficult to teach a dog social skills when they miss out on those early interactions with humans and other dogs. Difficult, but not impossible!

Each of us are presented with choices. We have the choice to allow our past challenges to define the future or we have the choice to heal and reach beyond what we ever thought possible. Gabriel, the angel dog, soared as he put his past behind him. He stayed with us for about a year, and he now lives in his beautiful forever home with his veteran, a partner for life ... knowing he is safe in the world and will never be placed in a kennel again.

26 Marathons and My Trainer

Jo Dibblee

My love affair with adoption and rescue started the day I walked into an animal shelter at age 19. Seeing the longing and the sadness of the dogs as I passed by each kennel broke my heart. I wanted to take them all home. For 38 years, I've adopted and rescued animals – cats, dogs, rabbits, etc. — and as a result, I've been the recipient of endless love, empathy, and adoration. That's what animals do, some more than others. Ironically, those who have endured the most abuse often give the most love. And this is particularly true with dogs.

Unlike humans, dogs seek belonging and service. Whether they're purebred or mixed breed, purchased or rescued, they long to belong and contribute to the pack. In everything they do, dogs show what it means to be fully present and alive. They show up in service, wanting only to be loved and to return that love. Always ready to play, they will howl and dance with you without worrying what anyone thinks.

They require no grand gestures; they love you for you, despite all your perceived and real shortcomings. For a simple bowl of kibble, a pat, a smile, and a game of fetch, humans become their everything.

In dogs, I've found the purest example of selflessness. They listen to our rambling thoughts as though we are spouting great genius, tilting their heads, and inviting us to continue. Or they keep us company by simply laying curled at our feet. Perhaps that's why their lives are so much shorter – they live so deeply and fully that what takes humans 60+ years to live, they can accomplish in 10 or 15.

I know some people think an over-attachment to animals borders on crazy. But for me, these beings create moments of transformation and joy like no other. Like us humans, dogs can be goofy, and each has a unique personality. But more than that, dogs are merciful and full of grace.

They know how to forgive.

All of this is even truer of rescue dogs, who, when adopted, are all in. There are so many beautiful dogs waiting for a forever home — dogs, who through no fault of their own have been re-homed due to unforeseen circumstances such as illness, relocation, or worse — dogs who are simply abandoned.

Yet, despite often experiencing the worst of humanity, these dogs somehow learn trust. Look no further than the dog who has been abused or abandoned and his or her willingness to approach a would-be Good Samaritan. Even dogs who are terrified due to past mistreatment will eventually soften with time and affection. Dogs tend to see the best in us humans and bring that out of us.

Dogs make a home richer. They make life better.

There came a day I knew my family needed a dog in our lives. I began looking to adopt a rescue dog, to complete our family. Every weekend for what seemed like forever, I went to shelter after shelter, and it was hard to walk away empty-handed each time. Even harder than walking away empty-handed was seeing the faces of the dogs who stared longingly into my eyes.

At the time, my children were young, and we were an active family. I was an avid runner and was training for a marathon. I wanted a running partner who wouldn't complain about running at 5 a.m. on cold, rainy days, one who would be ready to go whenever I laced up my running shoes and who approached running as I did, with joy and excitement.

I met Cassie, an eight-month-old puppy who had been abandoned not once but twice in her short lifetime, and was about to be euthanized due to lack of space. There was an instant heart connection, and we adopted her.

Cassie was fiercely loyal to the kids and me, and her herding skills became very handy. I would call the kids when dinner was ready, and Cassie would spring into action and round them up. She would run to the yard or wherever the kids were playing, gently put her mouth over each of their wrists, and guide them into the kitchen, as if to say, "Let's go! It's dinnertime!" It was something to see.

After Cassie's first birthday, we began running short distances. Cassie would run with me for the next eight years, and she was the best trainer I ever had.

Cassie had an uncanny sense of timing. Even before the alarm sounded, Cassie would be up with her head resting on the mattress, staring intently at me as if to will me to open my eyes. I could feel her gaze and, try as I might not to smile, how could I not? Her enthusiasm was contagious.

I knew as soon as I opened my eyes, the cozy cocoon that was my early morning bed would quickly disappear and so I would stay still, hoping for just a few more minutes. But once the alarm sounded at 5 a.m., it was mayhem. Cassie would jump on the bed as if to say, "Get up, get up! It's time to go!" I would dress, lace up my shoes, drink my tea, and off we went into the wee hours of the morning.

In the winter months, it was dark, with only the glow of the streetlights above to guide our way, and in the summer, despite the sun being up, we were often the only ones on the street. We did this for eight years. Rain, shine, snow, hail, sleet? It didn't matter. This was our time.

Cassie had an uncanny way of knowing exactly when I was lagging or not focused, and in true trainer fashion, when running on the leash, she would make any necessary corrections. Whenever I was dragging, Cassie would grab the leash in her mouth and, looking slyly at me, tug slightly to one side as if to say, "Come on, Mom. Enough lollygagging!"

Cassie knew what I was capable of, and I knew there was no escaping her demands. After all, I had also trained her well! And she was right.

As much as I enjoyed running distance, every marathon without fail I would hit the proverbial wall. My legs would seize up — the lactic acid burning as though my legs were on fire. Putting one foot in front of the other was torturous in those moments, and I would vow never to run another marathon. Of course, like any true marathoner, there was no way I was going to quit, either. I was too stubborn. Instead, I wished a car would hit me. Seriously!

It was in those grueling moments that I would recall Cassie running alongside me, slyly looking up, grabbing her leash, and tugging just enough to say, "Come on, then." And off I would go, knowing finishing was my only option.

I credit all 26 marathon medals to my training partner, Cassie. Just thinking about her on all those training runs was all that was needed to give me that second wind.

Cassie would be with us for eleven years.

I will never forget the day Cassie passed. How could I? I had known for weeks what had to be done. The vet had tried everything. Nothing we did was easing Cassie's pain. She could no longer stand up, sit down, lie down, or even lie still without whimpering. She was in so much pain. Arthritis had taken over her 11-year-old body, and I knew I had to do the "right thing" — the humane thing — but it was heartbreaking.

Cassie seemed to know this would be our last car ride. She looked at me with her big, brown eyes one last time as if to say, "It's okay." My heart hurt, and tears streamed down my face. I didn't want her to go, yet I didn't want her to hurt anymore. I stayed with her for 30 minutes after the vet said she was gone to thank her for all she did for me, for us, and all those who had met her. Cassie was so much more than a dog to me.

Leadership in Flight

Haseena Patel

I looked into those eyes, wide and curious. I felt a responsibility for its well-being – not only for its physical condition while it was in my care, but also for the energy that I brought to this beautiful bird. I felt love and life pulsing through the warm body of the yellow-masked weaver as I started to measure its beak length with the calipers. Next, I measured its wing length and tail. I consciously projected love energy while carefully placing a ring on the bird's leg, a recording and iden- tification process known as bird ringing. My friend, a licensed bird ringer, stood next to me, supervising. The best part of the process came next – releasing the bird.

It is a joy to watch a bird feeling its freedom and taking off into the spacious blueness above. What is it like to know the value and feel- ing of freedom so completely? How does it feel to trust in the process of flight with nothing but sweet-smelling, clean air to support you?

Until a few years ago, birds scared me, especially when they spread their wings. I didn't understand them, and I had no idea how to com- municate with them. What did we have in common? I didn't speak their language or know how to care for them.

But I had an epiphany one day when I recognized, through my experiences with them, that birds are beings, too. I am a different species, but I realized I can still treat any being of any species with love and respect.

That's the first lesson that bird ringing taught me. Leadership lesson one: All creatures give and receive love as a natural function of who they are.

Fear is at the root of behavior that is not loving. When holding a bird, it only attempts to bite my finger in a moment of feeling defenseless and fearful. We can apply this to human beings, too. Hurt people hurt people. When people are afraid of pain and vulnerability, they lash out in anger. Calm the fear, and the natural function of love prevails.

Leadership lesson two: Let there be purpose!

It was in 2015 that my friend invited my family and I to observe bird ringing. She was helping to ring a group of falcons that migrate from Russia to Newcastle, South Africa (the town where I live) every year. The ring enables us to track a bird, wherever it is in the world. One is able to access data about where it was ringed, its breeding habits, what stage of development it was in at the time of ringing, and approximately how long it has lived to date. With these details, we are able to know how to care for specific bird species as well as how to protect endangered bird species.

Where there is purpose, there is interest. I was always happy to tag along when my friend did bird ringing. I knew we were making a difference. I'd write down the pertinent information about the bird and have a great experience out in nature where I didn't have to check the time and used my phone solely to take pictures of different birds. I could do something that mattered while taking care of my mental and emotional health.

Leadership lesson three walked silently into my awareness: Allow the learning to touch your life.

I enjoyed being in nature – it was a change from my routine. During our bird-ringing sessions, I'd have fun working up an appetite and feasting on tea, boiled eggs, cheese, and cherry tomatoes, tasting edible plants, drinking from a stream with good water, breathing clean air, and spending time with my friend. Then, something within me shifted.

I don't remember when it happened, where, how, or why. I started learning more about birds in general and seeing the similarities in our ways of being. When a bird bit me because it was afraid, I stopped feeling afraid of being bitten. When we are stressed, we experience "tummy turbulence." It may sound unusual, but this realization that birds feel that, too, stopped me from being grossed out when a bird relieved itself on my hand. Instead, I felt compassion for the bird. Slowly, the barriers came down. I learned to trust in myself and in the birds I was helping to ring. This was where the communication began.

Leadership lesson four: Communication is about your energy, not your words.

Trust inspires confidence, and my newfound confidence had a ripple effect. I know the birds sensed it. All sentient beings sense one's emotions and deepest intentions. There aren't always words for this feeling, and as human beings, we don't always give credence to it. But that sense is always there – call it intuition in the human experience or simply communication through energy.

At least once a year, my friend gathers a group of children and includes them in the bird-ringing process so they learn about nature conservation and how to treat birds. I've been privileged to help educate the children during these sessions. They observe the process and get to release the bird after it has been ringed. It is a pleasure to watch children who are nervous about holding the birds grin with pride after they step out of their comfort zones and release the bird into the air. I enjoy empowering these young people to get comfortable with being uncomfortable and to grab every new opportunity they can with both hands. The energy I bring to their space has an effect on them. They sense my confidence and trust in it. They lean on my belief in them, and they gradually find their own confidence and self-belief. I see it in their eyes. They stand taller, they're not afraid to physically take up space and be, and they express themselves more vocally.

Enter leadership lesson five: Be open to the nudges from the Universe.

I wear a bracelet on my wrist that reads, "Everything happens for a reason." My truth is that I create my reality through my thoughts. Everything does happen for a reason – I create experiences that support my thoughts, beliefs, and deepest intentions. When my friend invited me to my first bird-ringing experience, I said yes – yes to her and yes to the Universe. I was open to a new experience that I intuitively knew would be good. I didn't know what I'd learn or that my fear of birds would transform into an understanding that we have the ability to communicate, collaborate, and connect with every being beyond our differences. I was open to the learning and stepped out of my comfort zone willingly.

It is in stepping out of all we think we know about ourselves that we forge a path in UN-becoming who we are not. This trail we blaze has the seeds of our evolution in it. Our path may begin with something as simple as a bird that scares us, but through our evolution, our fear dissolves, and we learn that the world is waiting for us to create, collaborate, connect, and commune. So we step out of our comfort zone and gift our presence to the world. That transformation is known as leadership.

Leadership is the intention to be in creation, collaboration, connection, and communion with the world and all beings in it; to learn, expand one's consciousness and evolve through such communication with one's world; and to gift this energy of expansion and evolution to one's world.

Connection Action Steps

1. Who is that friend or family member or neighbor or co-worker you haven't spoken with enough recently? Everyone has people they see or talk to all the time and those they care about but communicate with less often. Take a moment to reach out and renew that connection, even if it's something simple like a text.

2. Consider volunteering for an organization that supports animals and/or people who have experienced traumas or hardships. If you have experienced the same or similar traumas, your empathy will be a comfort to others and can open up a connection of understanding.

3. Dedicate time – even 5 minutes a day – to visualize a desired outcome in a situation or to reflect in gratitude about something or someone in your life (even your fur babies!). Your peace of mind through the contemplation may bring something positive to fruition, give clarity on a conundrum, or just feel good. If you are lucky, your animal companion can be there with you, too!

Affirmations

It is enjoyable to connect with others, with animals, and with my inner self.
I deserve to have meaningful connections.
I welcome the pure love that animals share and do my best to return it.

Journal Prompts

To connect with animals, we look beyond words. How do you communicate with the animal companions in your life? How do you see and know they are communicating with you? Describe the ways they communicate with you.

Connections are a part of the cycle of life. We are all born, and we will all die. What we do in between these times is what matters. Are we living a connected life that includes gratitude and unconditional love? How do you demonstrate your connections? List three ways you may invite more connections into your life, with both people and animals.

What deep, soulful connections have you experienced with humans and animals? Unconditional love is perhaps most freely expressed in our relationships with animals. How has an animal shown you unconditional love? Do you have a friend or pet who was in your life only a short time but the connection holds meaning to this day? Or maybe an animal who was in your life for a long time and taught you lessons about love, compassion, and appreciation. Write your story.

Love and Loss

'When you are sorrowful look again in your heart, and you shall see that in truth you are weeping for that which has been your delight.'
~ Kahlil Gibran

I am so grateful to have had many animals in my life. Looking back, I realize they taught me many things about myself and others. The compassion and hard work I learned from them inspired me to help as many people and animals as I could.

The loss of our animals is one of the hardest things to talk about, as their presence is so deeply missed. Every day they are our support systems, companions, and bundles of love. When we have no words to share or nothing else to give, they gift us with presence.

Before the creation of this book, we brought a new dog into our home that has provided love and fun. Yet, close to the completion of this book, I lost another dog we had for 16 years that provided so much love and companionship for my children. Both of these beloved pets showed us how to love better and more fully, how to trust, how to be in the moment, and how to play. I honestly believe animals teach us how to be more human! My heart is so big because of both the love and the loss of animals. Just when I think my heart can't grow any larger, they show me I always have room for more.

Lead with Love

Kate Neligan

As a child, I wanted to be a vet when I grew up because I loved animals more than anything in the world. I knew deep down, however, that I couldn't ever do that because I was terrified of blood. Just the sight of it made me feel as though I would pass out. Thirty years later, I found myself caring for my dying best friend, Felici, a beautiful and regal 17-year-old grey Arabian mare. Her name meant "happiness," and she showered everyone around her with it.

One day I stood outside her paddock holding her lead rope in one hand and cleaning the softball-sized melanoma tumor on her tail with my other hand. As large streams of red ran all the way down my arm, I paused and remembered how terrified I used to be of blood. I was surprised that I wasn't disturbed by it. I had a lifechanging moment then as everything stood still, and I realized I loved this horse unconditionally. Her blood and tumor were part of her so even they were beautiful to me.

A few years ago, about a month before her health took a turn for the worse, we were practicing a liberty walk, which is a ground-work-based exercise in an open arena, and my intention was to sync our walk and then run together. I couldn't get her to join up with me and, as I sat down in the dirt, my inner critic started to attack. She said, "You are so bad at leadership!" I sat there feeling sorry for myself and noticed Felici had turned her back to me and stood in the corner. It felt like she was purposely ignoring me. I quieted my inner mean girl and suddenly I heard another voice that said, "Lead with love." As I turned around to look at Felici, she turned to look at me and I said, "Did you say that? Did you say, 'Lead with love?'" She started to nod her pretty, dish-shaped head up and down in a clear yes. She walked toward me and stood over me in a beautiful stance of friendship and protection. I could feel her energy dripping over me like a bath of love.

After she died, I reflected back and knew deep inside that horses are here on Earth to teach us and heal us if we let them. I've loved and ridden horses since I was a youngster, but I had no idea they had these special powers. As I stepped further into my partnership with them and embraced equine-partnered life coaching as my career purpose, I've had more moments of awe than I can count. Miracles are normal around horses. They make the invisible world visible. They also have taught me much about leadership. Most of the lessons are critically important and timely for humanity to wake up now. Many people don't know that the leader in the horse herd is often the female: the lead mare.

Horse herds move together in the wild with a focus on safety, comfort, food, and play. The herd trusts the lead mare to make wise decisions that benefit the entire group, making sure their basic needs are met. While the herd is a matriarchy, it is not a typical hierarchical structure like our American corporate structure where there is a better than/less than system of titles and pay grades. The horse herd is a synergistic system and is built on relationships. All roles are equally valued. The herd knows that when one horse hurts, the entire system hurts. I believe that what the lead mare embodies can be a role model for a new humanity, a new Earth. The horse teaches us what blended energies look and feel like. When we look at a 1,200-pound majestic creature, we see strength and power in her incredible bone structure, muscles, and fast speed. We know that at any moment a horse could hurt us. Yet, anyone who spends time with them also knows of their gentle nature, their soft nuzzling touch. Horses will often just stand with you, asking nothing and simply sharing their essence with you, bringing you into their world.

Many people experience deep feelings of unconditional love, goosebumps, and a release of stuck pain just being around horses in silence. I once coached a corporate team and set up a team-building goal for two likable salesmen. Their objective was to move a horse in an arena to stand between two poles on the ground. This would help them see how they show up on their sales calls and in their deal-making. They started to chase around a sensitive horse, and chaos ensued. They were getting nowhere fast. I asked the men if they had said hello to the horse first. They stopped, looked sheepish, shook their heads no, and went up to stroke the horse's neck. Then I asked them what was happening, and they said they didn't want to pursue the goal at that moment; they just wanted to feel the softness and connection. One of them got emotional as he understood the horse's silent teaching: "Lead with love." These men realized the next time they were on a sales call they could take time to build rapport and respect and not rush to just close a deal. The time to cultivate relationships would lead to better sales while also bringing more fulfillment.

For so long we have valued results over relationships, masculine over feminine, logic over intuition, thinking over feeling, and doing over being. Where has this gotten us? The lead mare exemplifies and embodies the AND. She is both strong and soft. Gentle and powerful. Fierce and loving. Bold and compassionate. Goddess and warrior. Yin and yang. She is complete and whole. She uses all of her power to lead, not just half of it. I can't help but wonder what would be possible if humanity did the same. The lead mare also makes healthy and wise decisions for the greater good of the entire herd. The stallion backs her up with his physical strength, and together they lead as a team. This means the mare eats first whenever the herd finds food. She intuitively knows what humans need to be reminded of, which is to "put your oxygen mask on first" so you can help others.

As women, we can learn from the mare and choose healthy food, get enough sleep and exercise, and create time for play so we are even better partners, parents, and colleagues. We can learn how to deal with upset. Stress is not the horse's badge of honor like it has become ours. In fact, horses know how to diffuse fear, anxiety, and stress in just moments as they stay in present, mindful awareness and relaxed alertness.

Horses also demonstrate healthy boundaries. A "no" is clear from a lead mare. She doesn't apologize for her choices or care what others think of her. She will not be pushed around, and she will not accept rude behavior as respect is vital in her culture. She trusts herself and stays strong to support a thriving herd. Applied to humans, this means what is good for the woman is good for everyone. This is why smart men understand the phrase, "Happy wife = happy life," and this is why cultures that value, educate, and employ women prosper. The lead mare also shows us that being big and great is not something to fear; it's something to rise up into.

My first mare was a rescued chestnut thoroughbred named Lindsey. She was going to be put down because she wasn't rideable, but, thankfully, I saw her gifts as a coach and healer. She was a very large horse and could be intimidating to people because of her size even though she embodied a great deal of gentleness. During a meditation with Lindsey, a client who was previously scared of horses had an "aha moment" when she realized that just because something is big and powerful doesn't mean it will abuse its power. True power is power with, not power over! This is a very different approach from current horsemanship and present-day society. Many of the trainings I attended in the past teach humans that to get a horse to partner with you, you must first make the horse run around until it submits to your dominance. What does this equate to in our human world? A system of dictatorship. An outdated fear-based model that works briefly because of force but is not true power. It's also not sustainable as fear diminishes us over time.

Thankfully, Lindsey refused to join up in the old way. She acted offended or ignored me if I didn't approach her with both love and a playful spirit. The second I moved into joy she was with me and wouldn't leave my side. It's the same with my clients. A horse often won't budge when someone is in their head or wanting control, but when they surrender to their heart and become present, a horse becomes a loyal partner. Horses mirror a system that works, one of magnetism, presence, and power, rather than force.

The new leadership training for horses and for humans has to be about rapport, respect, and results. I believe we are moving into a circle system of teaching and learning because wisdom comes from all places — and all voices are valuable. This is why being in nature and with a horse herd is so important because that innate intelligence has functioned long before we were on the planet. The millennials are also showing us that we can't assume we know better just because this is how it's always been done.

I always say I'm not a horse whisperer; I'm a horse listener because most days the horses have a lot more to teach me than I could ever teach them. So, if Felici and Lindsey could verbally speak our human language they might have sang this song lyric first recorded by Nat King Cole: "The greatest thing you'll ever learn is just to love and be loved in return." This is the path to happiness. I believe that now we are at a critical time in our history as a species when equality must reign. We are being called to become better humans and love-centered leaders. We are being called to live from our true nature.

Whether male or female, whether your role is a parent, entrepreneur, VP of a corporate team, or global leader, you can learn from the lead mare. It is time to embrace the feminine in ways we haven't before. I believe we will be a happier humanity if we learn to understand, value, and respect the horse and the feminine.

It's time to be the lead mare of your life. It's time to lead with love!

Spirit Animals

Stef Skupin

In 2001, I moved to Cape Town, South Africa. After almost a year of traveling through Thailand and Australia, using the money I had earned during my first few jobs as a young veterinarian in the United Kingdom, it had been easy to find a position as a small animal vet in Cape Town, one of the most stunning cities on Earth. I was happily working for a wonderful and supportive older colleague, Dr. Steve Kitley of Riverside Vet. I lived with friends in an old villa with rambling gardens in Constantia, a Cape Town suburb famous for its beautiful properties and vineyards. Life was amazing. I was feeling incredibly lucky and blessed. I was totally in love with Cape Town, ready to put down roots and stay. So, for the first time ever, I allowed myself to take on a kitten.

Don't ask how I ever ended up becoming a veterinarian! My father disliked animals in the house so the only animal that ever lived with us was a budgie that had escaped somewhere else and ended up in our garden. Luckily, I was allowed to take riding lessons and fell in love with horses, but I'd never had an animal of my own.

Powderpuff was adorable, a six-week-old fluffy, white and gray long-haired fur ball, one of the myriad that arrive in veterinary practices. She was shy and tiny. I bought the right food and toys, made sure she was vaccinated, and took her home. For the first few days she'd mostly hide. My rooms were extensive, and I had little furniture so she was probably feeling exposed in so much free space. My friends had two big dogs and a ginger tomcat, but they were living on the other side of the house. I took care to close the doors when I left, making sure she was safely locked inside. Slowly, Powderpuff got used to being with me, and I'd look forward to coming home to my little charge after work.

When she'd been with me for about a week, I arrived home one night to find the door open. I rushed into my room only to find her lying there, a tiny heap of fur, unmoving, and already cold. My heart stopped. I rushed to her and picked her up, not believing my eyes. My little one, my responsibility, my love, my baby – gone.

Just like that, she had left, leaving me with nothing but guilt and the pain of her loss. I sat on the floor cradling her, sobbing. Behind me, Mano, my friend's pit bull terrier, padded into the room, looking at me guiltily. He must have opened the door and chased her, caught her – probably not even meaning to hurt, but those teeth and jaws would have finished her quickly. I screamed at him and hit him and chased him out, and he slunk down the hallway, tail between his legs, utterly miserable.

And so my attempt at having a cat ended less than a week after it began. I buried her in the garden, and I refused to speak to Mano for a week. Being a veterinarian, I blamed myself bitterly for not having taken better care, not knowing better, not having been able to save her life, not having been able to protect her.

That night, as dusk slowly turned to night, I sat in my room and cried. My candle in the window was sending flickering lights into the room when in walked the spirit of a cat. It was clearly Powderpuff, although she was fully grown. She walked in with an air of being entirely at peace, entirely untroubled, and coming to let me know that all was well. She brought with her such serenity and such oceans of loving concern for me that even remembering it today, it splits my heart wide open and makes me weep with gratitude. She was only there for a few heartbeats, but there was no doubt – she would be in my life forever. Death could not end this love. Death might have taken her body, but her essence, this loving concern, would never be lost to me again. Her death had given her the power to break my heart open and touch my own essence and bind it to her spirit.

Powderpuff taught me about the finality of the death of a loved one, and in the same lesson, she taught me about death's power to open us to love and the realm of spirit, the realm of the infinite. It was a lesson that helped me countless times hold the grief of pet owners and gently suggest that there remains a connection to the ones we deem lost, a connection that is all the more pure and intimate because it is not hampered by the boundaries of a physical body. Powderpuff died so that I could learn this lesson early in my career and continue to draw strength from it. No other animal came to me so clearly, in almost physical form – but then, they didn't need to, because a door in my mind had been opened, a door that took me as surely beyond my scientific veterinary mind as any near-death experience of my own could have done.

Six years later, I was preparing to leave on my honeymoon, still living on the same farm in Constantia. My friends had emigrated to Europe, leaving me with the dogs Mano and Chica, the ginger tom Binki, and my own now three cats: Jet, Jewel, and Sipho. Mano never touched another of my cats. Little Sipho, a little ginger tom who had just recently arrived, would scamper between Mano's legs and eat out of his food bowl, with Mano wroofing at me to please take the cat out of his bowl. Mano was now 12 years old. He was getting old, sore, and recently had been sick. He slowly stopped eating. We couldn't find anything wrong with him. His former owners had been gone for just over a year, and maybe he was just pining for them; he was such a loyal dog.

Mano started wandering down into the garden, lying there listlessly, clearly getting ready to pass on. As there was nothing else I could do for him, and because I was leaving on my honeymoon, I put him to sleep that night so he wouldn't have to suffer. We buried him under the trees in his garden, the garden he'd spent all his life protecting. I knew I was doing the right thing according to veterinary lore, but a part of me wished I'd just allowed him to pass over in his own time. I felt guilty and selfish.

That night, as my husband and I were driving through the dark towards Namibia, Mano's presence came to me. And again, there was that overwhelming love and care, that deep knowing that all is well. Whatever disagreements we might have had in his life, whatever end I had given him, it now was all well. There was such a reassurance that I didn't have to worry, that he died in peace, that we were bonded by love, and that he, too, would be in my heart forever.

With him came absolute peace and surety that in matters of life and death, nothing can be amiss, however much we might believe otherwise. We are taken care of beyond what we understand, beyond this life and form. We believe ourselves to be such important actors in our lives, making life and death decisions, while really, we are guided and held. Locked in misery, we believe in our mistakes while really, in the grand scheme of life going on for billions of years, what we call mistakes are merely the steps we take to grow in whatever way life needs us to.

Yet, I am a slow learner.

Despite the strong presence of both these beloved animals after their deaths, I refused to interact with and entertain the notion of a spirit animal realm for another six years. I'd become a homeopath, a Reiki practitioner for animals, and I had embarked on a spiritual path, working to drop the attachment to thought, to the illusion of reality. Clearly, animals' soul journeys and spirit animals would only add to the burden of thought that I could be attached to so why would I add any more layers to a reality that is illusory anyway?

By now, I had twin daughters, and our little family had moved to live in a nature reserve four hours outside of Cape Town. The Groot Winterhoek will always have a special place in my heart. It is on a mountain range in the northern cape. Its landscape consists of aged gray rock, small rivers, and cape fynbos – an incredibly diverse mix of flowers, grasses, low bushes, and small trees in colors of silver, blue and blue-grey, green, sand, red, orange, yellow, white, black, and brown. It is HOT in the summers and cool and rainy in winter, but hardly goes to freezing. Just after we moved to the reserve, it burned down completely so that we were surrounded with a blackened waste-land for about six months, after which the new generation of fynbos began to grow.

In our fourth year in the Groot Winterhoek, a group of women ran a Vision Quest at the center where we stayed. I had been invited to partake, but I felt that my path was clear to me and I didn't need extra guidance. While the group was out in the reserve on a four-day, silent fast, they left their books in the communal kitchen. I was intrigued and opened one of them: Ted Andrews' *Animal Speak*. For anyone who likes a good story with archetypes, and who wants to feel more in tune with animals and the natural world, *Animal Speak* is a riveting read. Andrews makes the case for the symbolism of nature speaking to us about the glory and infinite possibilities of creation in any moment, if only we decide to look. He also speaks of shamanic journeys and the magic inherent in creation. Now, almost 10 years later, I still don't understand everything he says, but his book has become a constant companion. Through him, I feel closer to this Earth and all its beings. They speak to me, and I to them, in the language of love.

Back then, in the Groot Winterhoek, I maintained my position of not needing further guidance for another month or two, then I gave in and embarked on my own private vision quest and fast. I connected with my first animal spirit guide, the bear.

I had always had nightmares about huge bears trying to break into my house or pursuing me – terrifying creatures as big as houses that obviously were out to kill me and my loved ones. Once I connected with Bear Spirit Guide, these nightmares stopped, never to return. Bear is a guide for the spiritual journey, holding us safe as we strive and prepare for transformation. So in a manner of speaking, Bear had prepared me for death – the death of the "old me" so that the next part of me could come out. As a Spirit Guide, Bear held that same serene and peaceful energy that everything is well, coupled with immense strength and power. With Bear as my guide, I feel held and protected.

Another Spirit Guide that came was Spider. Spider is Grandmother to indigenous peoples, meaning she plays pivotal roles in the myths of creation and maintenance of the world. Spider is tied to the Fates, the three women who weave mankind's destiny, and as such, Spider guards the primordial alphabet and is a guide to writers. Needless to say, during my journey with Spider, I developed a deep connection with all spiders, always allowing them space in my house. This does not mean, however, that I don't keep a respectful distance from a Black Widow.

Just like human archetypes, the wild animals hold specific energies that can teach us about the astonishing diversity and wonder of this miraculous world. Over almost 20 years, I've had to say goodbye on the physical level to many animal (and plant) friends. As a veterinarian, I was instrumental in many deaths – a lot of them planned, others I was helpless to prevent. People mourn the short lifespan of our companion animals, necessitating this experience of love lost. I think their deaths are one of their greatest gifts to us first worlders in an age when we are so unconnected to it. In Western society's well-meaning attempt to protect our feelings, help us live longer, and give us more freedom, we are disconnected from death, and as a result, unprepared for our own. The certainty of death can be a great gift, liberating us from the self-imposed limitations of civilized life. Witnessing death, and losing a loved one, can open our hearts to a bigger reality, to a wider perspective, and to deeper peace and love that are not accessible during the mundane hours of our days.

If we allow the grief of loss and limitation to take us over, it can become a pathway, a gateway to the experience of infinite love. It's a love beyond words and description, no longer tied to form, and so greedy it will take over anything and everything in its path. It has no limit, and it tolerates no limit. In it, we find all we ever lost, because here, in it, we are as one.

"The wailing of broken hearts is the doorway to God." – Rumi

Country Life

Joyce Benning

What an amazing journey God has led me on, living a country life that allows me the opportunity to pursue my passion of loving and caring for animals. This journey started with growing up on a dairy farm in central Kansas. Helping milk the cows began at a young age with my dad building a ramp so I could see over the feed bunk to feed the cows during milking. A very special blue roan cow named Tammy was super gentle, and you could love and pet on her out in the pasture. Such country life fun!

Bottle-feeding baby calves was one of the many chores I did on the farm, along with helping feed the cows. Caring for calves at a young age taught me responsibility as they depended on me for feed. These lessons helped mold my work ethic to what it is today.

On our ranch, the cattle have switched from dairy cows to beef cattle. Spring means calving time, which is my favorite time of the year. Each little baby calf is a new miracle. I love watching the baby calves running and playing with each other.

Dollie is one of those little miracles I raised as a bottle calf. Her pasture while growing up was our yard. It was always funny when people would drive in and say we had a calf loose in the yard. I would reply, "I know. That's just Dollie, my yard ornament!" Dollie became a great lead cow as she got older, bringing a herd of cattle out of a pasture and down the road to home. She would follow me anywhere if I had a bucket of cubes, which is like candy to cattle.

Kitty cats are another part of country life. Milking time growing up was exciting for them as they knew they would receive a bowl of fresh milk as a treat. Ranch life today has kitties waiting at the door for us to play and feed them. They are such colorful little bundles of life! Their enthusiasm each morning gives you a smile and appreciation for the start of a new day.

My love for horses also started at a very young age. Dad loved them and made sure I always had horses to ride. Some of these horses were a little bit on the ornery side, and I now believe it was Dad's way of teaching me to be a better rider. Dad had a motto: "Don't worry if you fall off your horse. The ground will not open up and swallow you; it will always catch you." This motto has taught me in life that if you fall, just cowgirl up and get back on with life!

Horses have always been magical to me as they are one of the animals I have always turned to for answers. Tom was one of those magical horses. He was a beautiful Bay that would take care of his rider and do anything you asked him to do. I feel very blessed to have had him in my life until he crossed the rainbow bridge at the age of 34. I believe his spirit rides with me all the time! I currently have three magnificent horses whom I communicate with and love on each and every day. Each horse has opened my soul to experience life in numerous beautiful ways. They have taught me to enjoy the moment, to practice gratitude, to love myself and take time for myself, to have patience, and to lead with my heart.

Australian shepherd and blue heeler dogs were also my best friends growing up on the farm. Zek and Blue Boy were two of my best buddies, as they were Christmas presents from my dad. Buck was another awesome blue heeler dog in many ways, especially when it came to working cattle. He would bring the cows up for milking from the pasture and then sit in the back of the holding pen to bring cows into the barn as we milked. Love and friendship with dogs have been and always will be in my heart and a part of my life.

Our dog family currently consists of border collie crosses and heeler dogs. Groucho is my little red heeler who is truly my very best friend. He knows me better than anybody ever will. We communicate so much just by looking into each other's eyes. One of the many parts of life he has taught me is to live with faith and not fear, along with never giving up. Groucho experienced a challenge six and a half years ago that started a journey of caring for our animal family in a natural way. I have found challenges in life do happen for a reason, as they help us to learn and grow into being better individuals.

Animals are not just in my life – they are my life, as they are family! Giving loving care to cattle, horses, kitty cats, and dogs is who I am. I'm honored to be a host on the Divas That Care Network with my own talk show, Robust Lifestyles, which gives me the opportunity to connect with many women who share a love of animals and nature. These incredible women have proven to me that connecting and communicating with animals and nature truly makes my life whole. When we take the time to go inside ourselves and realize what our true heart is telling us, the universe brings beautiful human and animal friendships to share with us on this journey called life.

Expectations: People vs. Dogs

Katherine Jensen

On April 9, 2019, the love of my life, John, passed away from brain cancer. This was the hardest day of my life.

We have all felt the pain of losing someone, be it to death or circumstance. Along with that comes expectations of our peripheral view, meaning the people who influence us or put pressure on us to make different choices that would be more suitable for them.

I have two mini Australian shepherds: Storm and Odin. They are the only two souls in my life that have no expectations at all. None. One of the purposes that dogs have is to be present 100 percent of the time – no matter what.

During the seven months my husband struggled with this dreadful disease, we had a lot of people around and I was gone quite a bit. I worked full time as the owner of a busy and successful dog services company. Even though it was wonderful having people around, there was a lot of negativity that came with it, also. There were many people who shared their opinions, criticisms, and judgements of me. Some of these were passive aggressive, and some were just plain aggressive. The opinions and judgements I received were mostly about me working so much and not being at home to take care of my sick husband. However, when I was home, I was treated like an outsider by those that were around. That left me feeling angry, hurt, and frustrated. I couldn't believe this was even happening during this time of my life.

I am so very thankful for having Storm and Odin during those days. Storm and Odin didn't care how often I was away from home.

I could be gone 10 seconds or 10 hours, and those two would greet me at the door with their excited squeals. They always made me feel better and brought a smile to my face.

One thing I learned is that not every person's situation is the same. As an entrepreneur, I knew that just because my loved one was ill didn't mean work stopped. I had responsibilities to my clients and employees. My husband was dying, and I did want to spend as much time with him as I could, but at the same time, I had been working so hard on this dream and I couldn't quit, either. I was scared I would have nothing after all this.

The reality is, with Storm and Odin I'd never be alone or have nothing left. I'd always have them. My amazing dogs could feel my pain, anger, and frustration. They would sit on my lap for hours snuggling and laying down with me as I cried.

I am a strong, independent woman who learned over many years of trials and tribulations to deal with my issues in a positive way. I was in therapy for years, became a life coach, and learned yoga and meditation. I am thankful I had done that, and so when dealing with some of the negative individuals in my life, I was able to understand what was happening. What people didn't realize was I was gearing up to have everything in place at my business so that when all these individuals left, I could be home full time with him during the last days of his life. So that I could build those memories that I would have forever.

My dogs, Storm and Odin, gave me strength and love. Whatever path I chose, they were there by my side, walking along with me without a care in the world, trusting every decision I made. With animals, there is no judgement, blame, or resentment. This is something that I have learned over the years with many animals that I have had.

John knew me, he knew my passions, my life's work, and he knew how important keeping my business was to me. He complained from time to time, before he was sick, that I was a workaholic, but he never made me feel bad for dreaming and dreaming big. When he was sick, he never criticized me for wanting to carry my dream forward. I will love him forever because of that.

Now that he's gone, there is a hole in my heart that will never heal. When the wind blows through it, it kindly reminds me of the love we had and the love I lost way too soon. From all of this, though, I remained true to myself and what I needed to do for the survival of my business and the survival of myself after losing the love of my life of 23 years.

Storm and Odin were put on this planet to be my little Earth angels. When John passed away, Odin went over and sniffed him and laid on his bed. Storm was the most concerned of the two during the whole ordeal. He would always be watching and looking concerned. He would sleep at John's feet every single day just in case he was needed for something ... anything. The day my husband died, Storm jumped up on his lap and kissed his cheek ever so gently to say his goodbye.

From that moment on, it was the three of us, navigating this new life we found ourselves in. Coming home every night to a dark and empty house. No "Hello, baby" and "Hello, boys." The silence was deafening. I would walk around tiptoeing as if not to disturb the quiet. Storm and Odin would be curiously wondering why I whispered to them asking if they were hungry. Then the silence would break with the excitement of having dinner, with some dancing around and the little noises they make because they can't speak to tell me they couldn't be happier in that very moment.

I may have lost the love of my life, John, but I have two more that love me unconditionally, with no expectations. These dogs have taught me more about myself just by listening to them, watching them, and spending time with them. These two beautiful boys have given me more than I feel I deserve because they feel I deserve it. I couldn't imagine my life without them, although I know one day I will have to and my heart will break again, making two more little holes that that breeze will blow through, reminding me once again that I was fiercely loved.

After John passed, I went straight back to work. This was not the healthiest thing for me to do, but I felt I had to keep moving. Storm, Odin, and I had to find a new normal. This new routine that surprisingly felt like the old one, now had a missing pack member.

It wasn't easy to say the least. It seemed one bad thing after the other kept happening. From issues with the business and the death of a dog at the facility to dealing with new regulations that had to be incorporated.

Storm and Odin were with me every day all day. Working to take care of me. They followed me everywhere. Then, something started happening that I wasn't even aware of at first – they were becoming the type of dogs I took in to train. They became whiny and barky, and Odin was becoming aggressive to other dogs. I was devastated.

During this time, I had started binge eating and binge drinking. I would come home at night and eat unhealthy foods like pizza, and drink wine each night just so I could sleep. This led me to gain 70 pounds. I wonder why my dogs were acting out?

It's so funny how I talked earlier about others' expectations. I didn't even realize I had put so much pressure on myself, working 14-hour days, to become a foodaholic and a drunk. A dear friend helped me through this time of self-destruction, and I realized I needed to sell my dog services company in order to help with the healing process. Looking back, I see Storm and Odin were trying desperately to tell me I was spiraling out of control by acting out in bad behavior.

So I did it. I listed and sold my dream and didn't look back.

Not long after, I sold my house and moved away. During this time, a friend of mine and I decided to develop a healthier lifestyle. I had begun to really notice how self-destructive I had become and how my unhealthy decisions affected my dogs. I was so embarrassed by how far I had fallen.

One year after selling my dream, I had lost 47 pounds and had a healthier relationship with alcohol.

Storm and Odin are healthier, too. Overall, their behaviors have improved.

I am now inspired to go back to life coaching, writing, and doing some podcasting to hopefully help empower others by sharing my journey and interviewing others about theirs.

No matter how people have judged and put expectations on me, I have danced to the tune of my own drum. Even after a year of self-destruction, I went back to what worked for me. Walking in nature almost daily with Storm and Odin, yoga, and journaling. I also practice right action, kindness, and supporting my community and my "pack" as often as I can.

I would not be where I am today without my pack. My friends and, of course, my dogs! A post came across my social media one day from Ultimate Fighting Championship Icon Dana White, who said, "Surround yourself with people who brag about you, say your name in rooms of opportunity, hold you accountable with softness and love, celebrate your wins as their wins, have more compliments for you than shade, encourage new experiences and growth. This is the basic criteria. Assess your circle."

No matter what life throws at you, there are always people out there who will support you. Find those people! They could be a teacher, friend, therapist, or pastor. Or even maybe a dog. Whoever you find, make sure they meet the criteria and don't settle or allow others to make you feel small. Stand up, push your chest out, and let go of the need for approval. Live your best life, and no matter who is in your peripheral vision, ignore the noise, and be your amazing self.

Becoming the Community Cat Lady

Kathy Lynn Mackison

As a kid, our family had one German shepherd dog, Greta. My whole family went to the animal shelter to pick out Greta when I was young. The only thing I remember about that first visit to the shelter was there were so many animals. Some of the animals would come to the front of the cage and almost beg us to take them home. Others would just lie there. I remember thinking that if they could talk, they would say, "Why bother? No one picks me." Even though I was excited to have Greta, and really loved her, it took several days for me to get over the sense of sadness that I couldn't take all the animals home from the shelter. Thinking about the sad animals we left behind always hurt my heart.

Greta was our family dog when we lived in the country. She was very loyal and would follow my sister, Millie, and I as we rode our bikes. I remember her being protective of Mama and us kids. She was a beautiful girl and sweet. When we moved to the city, we didn't have room for Greta, and we had to leave her with the farmer next door. It was so sad to leave her behind, but it wouldn't have been fair to keep her locked up in the city after she was used to having so much freedom in the country.

In the city, we couldn't have another dog, but we were able to adopt a few cats. Sometimes one would turn up, and we would adopt it. The family favorite was Boots, a beautiful black-and-white tuxedo with the most perfect white "boots" for paws. I remember Boots being such a cool cat. He would let my little brother and sister drag him around without a complaint. He was a great snuggler and had the sweetest personality. We lost him when I was in high school. He was hit by a car when he was napping in the road (a habit we couldn't break him from).

If you would have asked me 20 years ago if I eventually would have 30 cats, I would have laughed you out of the room. At that time, I was in my 30's and super busy with work and traveling. If I did adopt a pet, it would have been a dog because I had such fond memories of Greta. Yet, I wouldn't consider adopting a dog because it wouldn't have been fair with my work and travel schedule.

Even though Boots had been a cool cat, I'd had bad experiences growing up with other cats that were not as well-tempered. My cousin Melissa had several ill-tempered cats that must have been able to sense I didn't care for them because they would attack me for no reason. This left me with a bad feeling about cats, and I had no interest in adopting them.

Fast forward to 2012. I was living in San Diego and working a stressful job as an accountant. After 17 years in accounting, I was burned out and frustrated, looking for an outlet where I wouldn't think about work. My friend Carol dared me into going skydiving. Even though I was afraid of heights, I wanted to do it. I wanted to push through my fear. From the first jump, I was hooked and from then on, I jumped almost every weekend. One of my first friends in skydiving was Grace, and she is the one who talked me into adopting my first cat, Natalia. I don't exactly recall what Grace said, but I know she planted Natalia into my heart somehow. I was still working around the clock and didn't have time for a cat, but I agreed to adopt her.

Natalia was a beautiful tortoiseshell (aka tortie,) but it took about two seconds for me to realize I didn't know anything about cats. Natalia hid in my basement, and I had to drag her out to get her into my room. Once in my room, she used under my bed as her home. I would literally crawl under my bed to feed her and pet her, waking up many nights with a backache and having to crawl back out. Eventually, Natalia jumped on the bed to sleep with me. I will never forget that night. I was so excited! Yet, even then I had to be super careful not to move too much because she was so skittish.

Natalia learned to trust me, and she became one of my best companions. She moved with me from California to Minnesota to Georgia, back to California, and eventually home to South Carolina. When I suffered from vertigo, she never left my side. When I struggled from burnout and depression, she never left my side. She was loyal and sweet. She would literally lie beside me all day long and never complain while I slept.

During our stent in Georgia, we added Howdy to our crew. Howdy was a tuxedo and such a sweet boy. He seemed to be happy all of the time. He and Natalia never really loved each other, but they learned to respect each other. And they became my buddies during some of the most stressful times in my life. I was working like crazy and miserable, only I didn't understand how truly lost and miserable I was. Natalia and Howdy would lie beside me for hours while I suffered from vertigo and frustration and depression. They were so loyal.

Roll forward to 2018, and we finally moved home to South Carolina. My grandparents had been sick, and it was time to return home. Eight states in 22 years was enough, even for a trooper tough as me. My awesome Aunt Mary came to California and drove with Natalia, Howdy, and me across the country. I was so happy to see California in my rear view. I was tired of moving back and forth across the country like a gypsy. I was ready to be home.

Natalia and Howdy lived with me and my grandparents when I first moved home and came to love my grandparents. But then Natalia started suffering from a weird brain disorder, and she stopped eating. I had to put her to sleep. To say it was hard is an understatement. She was such a sweet girl, and it had taken so long to win her over. Now we were finally home, and she had to go. Shortly after, within a month or two, Howdy disappeared. I could tell he was winding down … a cat mom just knows. A month or so before he disappeared, he started sleeping in my armpit under the cover. It was like he couldn't get warm. He knew he was about to cross the rainbow bridge, and it was his way of saying goodbye.

It was so hard to lose Natalia and Howdy in such a close time frame, but I felt it was Father God's way of showing me I was finally in the right place. Natalia and Howdy had been with me in the worst of times. They had lain next to me for hours as I was sick and struggling with depression, and they never complained. They traveled back with me to South Carolina. They left me in a better place than they found me. I will never forget those two loving kitties. They will always have a special place in my heart.

Yet, God has a way of bringing new love and life to a situation, and it didn't take long for more kitties to start turning up at Byrd Farm.

Mama Cat, a sweet and beautiful Persian mix, had been living on the farm for a while, and she brought us several lovely, little kittens. They were born on my green chair in the barn, and it was so special. Polar, Top Cat, Sweet Baby, Asia, Jasper, Fluffers, and Mama Cat would hang out with me in the green chair as I would read my Bible. It was so sweet how Father God sent me so many little babies after losing Natalia and Howdy.

Jasper and Fluffers were adopted, and I lost Asia one day when she was run over. I was out with Grandmother for the day and will never forget how Grandfather looked when he had to tell me. I cried for two days. I think it was all the stress of losing Natalia and Howdy and then Asia. It was like a well broke inside me. Mama Cat was run over shortly after. I started to feel like maybe I should give up on the kitties, but what choice did I have? Taking them to the shelter seemed so much worse. Just the thought of going to drop off any of my precious babies would bring back the childhood memories and tears.

It seemed there was no path but to become the "Community Cat Lady," come what may, to love them for as long as Father God sees fit to leave them here and then remember the good times and how happy they were on Byrd Farm.

Ever since this decision, the cat numbers on Byrd Farm have gone up and up. I had four pregnant mamas, and several more were dropped off. They are all blessings, and I praise God I have the opportunity to take care of His little creatures, as I have gained more than I have lost. I do try to keep them fixed, of course, although staying on top of it all can be hard at times.

Being a community cat lady is fun, challenging, heartbreaking, sad, and a lot of work but also rewarding in so many ways. Between strays, drop-offs, and our own pets, I have taken care of as many as 30 cats on Byrd Farm! Who knew this dog person would ever get to experience the love of so many cats?

Grief, Death, and Dying

Tracy Pierce

Ever since I was a young child, I have had a special connection with animals. Looking back, it's no surprise I eventually became an animal communicator. My first best friend was a miniature schnauzer named Pepper, and my parents delighted in taking photos of me and the dog drinking out of the dog bowl together or sharing a Milk-Bone®. As I grew up, we continued to have pets who lived with us – dogs and cats, mostly. And when we visited my grandparents' farm, we'd get to meet the cows, chickens, and maybe some baby kitties if we were lucky.

Animals have always played a part in my life, but it wasn't until my late thirties when Magoo, one of our three cats, got sick that I felt moved to listen to my animal friends on a deeper level. It was Magoo's illness that sent me down a path of learning animal communication, and each one of the three cats we had at the time played a major role in helping me remember how to communicate with animals.

It was primarily through these three cats' deaths that my learning deepened in ways I could not have imagined. In today's society, we often view death as a terrible thing, but my experiences with death have led to some of the biggest openings and spiritual connections of my life, and this precious death time window deserves to be honored for the gift it truly is.

Around the time Magoo first got sick, I met an animal communicator at a meditation retreat and decided to seek her services to help us with Magoo's health since the vet had not been able to conclusively tell us what the problem was. During those animal communication sessions, it felt to me like something was waking up inside of me, like part of me had always known how to communicate with animals. I started to remember long-forgotten memories of talking to animals as a child, but it felt like that part had fallen asleep over the years.

My husband and I did several sessions with different animal communicators as Magoo approached the end of her life. After a couple months of intense home care, she passed away at home while both my husband and I sat with her.

During this time, I was doing a lot of spiritual and meditation practices, and I was starting to "see" things happening on an energetic level, such as the energies that surround people and animals. Although Magoo's passing was difficult, there was so much to see around the transition time of her leaving her body. I felt like I gained a deeper understanding of death by going through this experience.

About a year later, one of our two remaining cats, Zella, became ill. When I teach animal communication courses, Zella often wants to assist me with the class. I consider her one of my animal communication teachers, and during the last three months or so of her life, her voice began to come through so strongly that I no longer needed an outside animal communicator to relay her messages to me.

She taught me much about myself, and she highlighted some of my old patterns in my life that I was replaying with her. It was unbelievably eye-opening to have her reveal so much of her own perspective on my own life and the connection the two of us shared during those last weeks of her life. Even though it was an incredibly difficult time, it also felt like a time of deep learning.

I got the sense of her energy starting to unravel, especially the five or so days before her death. She started to show me memories of things from our past from her viewpoint. I got the sense that she wanted me to acknowledge that I saw and understood the impact that those events had for her. There were things about our past that she wanted to get off her chest before she left. She didn't want to leave any unfinished business between us.

Furthermore, Zella made it very clear how she wanted her death. She asked for the same homeopathic remedy Magoo had been given that helps speed up the death process. The vet had informed us with Magoo that a pet dying at home can be a traumatic experience for both the pet and the owner, and she wanted us to be fully informed of what a pet dying at home can entail. It can take up to two weeks for a pet to die once it stops eating and drinking, and it can be difficult or impossible to give them pain relief after a certain point because of decreased circulation and organ function. And once an animal's circulation drops to a certain level, euthanasia is no longer an effective option. Luckily, our vet was also trained as a homeopathic vet and was able to give us a remedy that speeds the dying process up to two or three days.

During those last few days with Zella, she was clear on what she wanted. It was like she was giving me an instruction notice for her death. She wanted to die at home with us there. She wanted to still be able to sleep near me so I made adjustments to my bedroom so we could do that since she could no longer jump up on the bed. She made it very clear when she was done eating food or drinking water.

When it got to the point she could not walk anymore, there were times she wanted to be left alone in the bedroom and there were times she wanted us to be with her. She told me that sometimes she felt overwhelmed by the level of our human sadness as she was getting ready to leave and needed some space from that. I noticed in my own energy that when Zella and my etherics (the life force energy that runs in and around all living beings, sometimes known as chi or prana in other traditions) would touch each other, I felt deep sadness. I got the sense of my own physical attachment to having Zella with me in the physical world and how sad it made me to realize she was leaving.

I saw that many of the things I thought I wanted to do to help Zella with her transition were more about comforting me than comforting her. For instance, petting her. After a certain point, Zella said she did not need to be petted as much as I thought she did, and she asked me to be more aware of whether I was petting her for her or petting her for me.

Additionally, she showed me how keeping the focus on what is comforting to her would be a huge part of what could help ease her through this transition gracefully. She wasn't asking me to ignore my

own feelings, just to be aware of how (and where) I might be expressing them and asking myself whether those expressions were helping
or hindering her transition.

Even though there were times she wanted to be alone, there were
also times she wanted one or both of us in the room with her. There
were a few times when I got the ping from the other room that she
felt scared and now wanted someone to sit and be with her and talk
to her a bit.

Zella started to noticeably transition out of her body the day before she actually passed. I could feel her energy starting to lift out of
her physical body. The previous couple nights, I sensed her energy
moving around the room more freely; her energy felt less attached to
her physical body. It felt like she was walking around on the bed and
the room, even though she was not able to move much physically at
that point.

There was such a huge heart space emanating from and around
our sweet Zella. So much warmth and golden light filled the space. We
did our best to open to the bittersweetness of the pain of her leaving.

During this time, I also sensed the presences of two of our cats
who had passed previously, Magoo and Seeker. It felt like they were
holding space for all of us from non-physical realms and that they
helped the process of Zella leaving her body in the end. Both my husband and I thought we had seen and/or felt both Magoo and Seeker
wandering around in the house the days before Zella's passing.

Zella had forewarned me that there would be a time close to her
actually leaving her body when it looked like her physical body was
still alive, but she did not want anyone to touch her anymore at all.
She said that us touching her made it harder for her to leave the physical body; she wanted us to just sit and hold the space for her to leave
without touching her.

And we did that. My husband and I sat in the room with her and
held space as it became clear that her death time was nearing. It was
an incredible space, the presences of angels there to assist with the
transition process were extremely tangible – and they held us all in
the space of divine white and gold light as we felt the slow process of
Zella's spirit leaving her physical body.

There was a moment during her actual transition when I felt like the guardianship of Zella was passing from me back to the Universal Mother. Shortly after, we were inundated with light, and Zella's energy was uplifted and pulled from her body. I opened my eyes to look at her body, and although she was still taking very small sips of air, it felt like it was only her nervous system, that there was no spirit in her body any longer. In a few moments, all bodily functions seemed to cease.

We kept Zella's body with us for a day or two after she passed. We had hoped to keep her for three days before taking her to be cremated, but it was a hot August in a humid climate and after one and a half days it became clear we needed to take her body to the cremation facility.

Although Zella had given me a fantastic education through the death process, her teaching did not stop after her departure from the physical world. In my experience, it can be difficult to connect with an animal for communication right after death, but this is not true in all cases. Zella had appointed herself as one of my teachers in the matter of death from an animal's perspective, and she made it a point to show me things every day after her passing to help more thoroughly educate me in matters of what happened to her after her physical death.

I noticed that I could still feel Zella's etheric energy around her physical body even after she had passed. Every time I would get close enough to her body that our etherics touched, I would feel waves of sadness wash over me, but once I would move away, I would be fine. I had read that in some esoteric teachings, it is said it takes the etheric energy of a being a few days, typically three, to dissipate or "fall apart" since it has some attachment to the physical body. I had read that other layers of our energy are able to leave this plane much more easily. It was interesting to see these principles in action after Zella's passing.

We also noticed that the presence of the other cats, Magoo and Seeker, left almost immediately after Zella's passing, like they were here for a specific mission and then they left again. The day after her passing, Zella's energy felt quite cloudy, and there was a sense of chaos when I tuned into her. Then, about 40 hours after her death, I could feel her presence bright and shining, almost like a star.

I kept tuning in as the days went by. I felt her energy go through different phases. It often felt like her energy was being washed, rearranged. This continued for the better part of two weeks before she felt like she was more fully integrated into the spirit world.

Zella has continued to show me things since her death and has become one of the primary animal friends who helps me teach animal communication courses. She is always eager to be a part of the process of animal communication learning.

Although I consider Zella one of my primary animal communication teachers, I would be remiss not to mention the third cat who lived with us during the time I was learning animal communication – Captain Malcolm Reynolds – or Mal for short. Mal also wanted to teach me about death.

During the time that Mal became ill, my husband and I were living separately. I was in Colorado doing some recon as to where we wanted to move, and my husband was still living in Iowa with Mal. As Mal's health declined, I spent many hours communicating with her with the help of my animal communication practice partner, Nina. Mal told us that she, too, wanted us to learn about what happened to an animal spirit as it made the transition through death.

Mal was scheduled to be euthanized, and Nina and I tuned in during her appointment time. Mal had also asked that we try to connect with her every day for two weeks after she passed. We did this, and Mal showed us all the transitions she moved through, and when she could, she told us about her own experiences. Part of what she wanted to show us was that death was simply another transition, not something to be afraid of.

Although she could not communicate to us in the same way she had when she was alive, Mal did her best to impart to us what her experiences were right after death. Her communication felt different immediately after death compared to what it was like before and compared to what it was like about a week after her passing. In my experience, there seems to be a window of haziness immediately after death wherein it is difficult, if not impossible, to communicate with the recently deceased in an effective way.

Although I miss them in the physical world, my connection with these cats became stronger after their passing. It was almost as if a new relationship with them was born through their deaths. I learned so much about animal communication through my connection with these three cats. They brought themselves forward to be my teachers; I only had to accept their help to be taken to the next level.

In fact, I find now that one of the primary reasons people come to me for animal communication is because a pet is approaching death or has recently passed. Because of my experiences with Magoo, Zella, and Mal, I am able to provide deeper support for both the animals who are passing and their humans.

Our animal friends can become such a special part of our lives, and it's rarely easy to let them go. However, this "training" that my kitty friends have given me about death has changed my perspective completely. Animals don't think of death the same way that humans typically do, and I am deeply thankful for the education my dying cats gave me. I would not have the same understanding of animal communication without them.

Horse, Heart, and Home

Ley-Anne Mountain

I have always found my answers with animals. They have always been my safe place. They are my guides for learning. As a child, my personal boundaries were unheard, disrespected, crossed, and broken, which caused me to have a deep-rooted belief that humans had failed me. Experiences I had no say in or control over left me doubting my own species. My ability to trust humankind became a journey I made alongside animals. My animals carried me through ... literally.

It was one animal in particular who gave and taught me courage, love, patience, and respect. That animal was Cougar, my first horse. It was a blend of caring for him and becoming a mom myself that led me on my path to finding my way back to my human herd.

At the tender age of 16, I finally got my very own horse. My first horse, my first love. A Christmas present that arrived with every bit of magic and wonder you expect a dream come true to have. I had been working at a stable for a few years and, at last, I had a horse of my own.

Cougar and I had 10 wonderful years together. In those years, he supported and led me through the growing pains of a teenager becoming a young adult. Life-changing events like graduating high school, my parents divorcing, moving out of my childhood home, and heading off to college. We traveled everywhere together, from horse shows to riding clinics. We were never apart.

I always had to board Cougar. I, too, felt like I was always "boarding" somewhere. I hadn't felt like I had a home since leaving the acreage after my parents' divorce. Then, in college, I met my husband Mark and we moved to Innisfail, Alberta, shortly after graduating. In December of 1999, Mark and I purchased our first home. A brand-new mobile home with a beautiful space for a pasture for my Cougar. Being winter, Cougar would have to wait to "come home" until we could build a fence for him in the Spring. On the May long weekend of 2000, I finally brought him home. We officially had a home.

Together. Both Cougar and I would never have to board anywhere ever again.

"Mark, please can you take a picture of us? We are home."

Exactly one month to the day after our picture was taken, Cougar died. For 30 days of our 10 years, we lived together at our home. Before our paths crossed, I had no idea how powerful and life-changing our time together would be for me. No idea how many life lessons he would teach me. And no idea how broken and empty I would feel when he was gone.

It was in his life that I learned. I learned responsibility by caring for another. I learned friendship, partnership, love, non-judgement, honesty, security, and trust. I learned what it was to feel safe. He showed and offered me courage. It was on his back that he carried me safely back to humanity. Nothing phased him, NOTHING. Except for one thing ...

We were getting ready for a horse show. I had just finished bathing him and tied him to a hitching rail to dry in the morning sunshine. One thing to know about Cougar is that he was a professional at untying himself and any other horse around him. No exceptions! After tying him up, I went into the house to shower. In my fluffy pink housecoat, towel wrapped around my head, I peeked out of the window to check on him. Surprise, surprise, he had untied himself!

I ran outside to catch the escapee before he decided a dirt bath was on the agenda and, well, he took one look at the fuzzy, pink maniac running towards him and took off running! To this day, I still have a smile on my face when I remember it. I settled myself down after I realized how scary I must have looked to him, housecoat and towel flapping all over the place! He was definitely dry after that run around!

The pain and sadness I felt when Cougar died and I lost him forever was unlimited, endless. Grief and guilt were held in every cell of my being and in every tear that fell unexpectedly from my eyes. I couldn't speak his name without a tremble from my lips. I felt responsible for his death. IF I had called the vet earlier, IF I wasn't working that day. IF I followed my gut that there was something wrong. Could I have done more to help him? Looking back now, I did everything possible at the time. I did call the vet and get medications to help him. I did call the vet again when things got worse within the hour. We did perform surgery and everything else possible that could save him. The vet left at 3 a.m. I stayed up with Cougar all night. At 5 a.m. I made the decision to euthanize my horse. It was also Father's Day. We did everything possible to save him and he died. Horse or human, there is no evaluation scale of who or what we love. This is where I feel I learned the greatest gift life gives us.

The grief from Cougar's passing was the final lesson he had for me. Everything he had taught me during his life is what I needed to walk through his death and come out the other side, healed and ready to start a new journey, a new chapter. It was navigating Cougar's death that changed my path in every possible way. It was during this time that I found Craniosacral Therapy as I was held in compassion and in human hands to help release and accept the painful story of grief. Through every moment, I was held and supported by the other animals in our herd. C-Fer, the cat, and Crash, our border collie. Yet I wasn't only supported by our animals but by the land, too. Our Mother Earth who catches our every footstep. Who feeds us, nurtures us, and loves us. There is also my human herd.

If something is alive, it will die. Such is the circle of life. There is nothing easy about experiencing loss. Whether it's the loss of someone or something we love, be it a pet or a person, a home, a marriage, or even one special moment of time in our life. Even feeling the loss of a favorite cup as you drop it and see it broken into a million pieces on the floor.

I believe each and every animal on this planet is unique. No matter the species, they offer unconditional love without judgement. That is the gift that they so freely offer us and if we are open to accepting it, it will help us heal. They teach us skills through body language, compassion, empathy, and tolerance, and it is these skills that can be applied to any and all relationships, be they animal or human. Nature, too, talks to us, constantly.

While finding my way back to my whole self, I realized that I never really lost it. Being human is feeling lost in moments, found in moments, sad in moments, and happy in moments. It also means having love for each moment, even the ones I would rather forget. Honestly, sometimes I feel I have myself on the end of a lunge line running circles trying to figure things out.

Whoa … From the wings of my angel, Cougar, messages of unconditional and timeless love still make their way down an invisible path seeping into my heart. Leading and guiding me to be as kind, patient, and compassionate with others and myself, as my animals are with me. Sometimes, I forget to put myself on the list. Kids, husband, animals, garden, clients, friends – all on the list. Cougar reminds me of me. Thank you, Cougar.

Animals remind me of the truth in, "Home is where the heart is," and I am home because of them.

When Fate Brings You Fur Kids

Jean Brannon

"Say what?"

I gaped at my phone. At the words my eldest nephew had just uttered. At the incredible ridiculousness that had already begun to unfold.

"I said I brought two starving puppies to my apartment, Aunt Jean. But my cats hate them."

"So, you want me to take them?"

"Welllll." Charlie laughed. "Yes."

Ah, that little word, "yes." I knew if I said it, I was adding a whole new sideshow to the three-ring circus taking center stage in my life. I mean, I'd recently moved. Started a business venture. Begun working on a fixer-upper that was nearly beyond fixing. And I'd been writing, deliriously absorbed in a sequel that kept pulling me into another world for hours at a time, all while getting the two shelter dogs I already called "fur family" comfortable in still-unfamiliar territory.

"It could be fun," Charlie suggested. He said it so cheerfully. So convincingly.

"And it could be what finally makes me go crazy," I sighed.

"You know, they're a bonded pair," he continued, sensing me weakening. "Maybe three months old. Brother and sister. They go to sleep hugging each other."

"Oh, dear." My resolve crumbled further as he sent me the first picture. And as he began telling me what he knew about the quiet boy and his scruffy sister with one blue eye who seemed to have been on a mission for weeks to reach me.

Oh dear, indeed.

Finding Puppy Love in a Most Unusual Way

My nephew Charlie is in college, and his school had sponsored an adopt-a-thon with a local animal shelter. And so, on a rainy spring Saturday, Charlie sloshed his way through a town park to support this "fur-ever home" project. It wasn't long before he noticed a scrawny black puppy by his side. A puppy with one floppy ear, one eye the color of icicles and the other eye as dark as night. Ribs poked and parted her dull coat. Yet she licked his hand enthusiastically whenever he bent to pet her. And she stuck to his side like raggedy Velcro as he perused more than 20 cages of wet noses and whiny barks.

At one point, Charlie sat with a friend near the cages who asked if he'd adopted her. My nephew replied that he hadn't, but as she curled herself into his lap, he realized she had already claimed him.

As Charlie pondered his options, he said to his friend that he should probably start by finding out if any of the shelter folks knew anything about this puppy he'd already nicknamed Blue Eye. Gently, he placed her on the pavilion's cement floor so he could begin his detective work. And she darted out into a downpour. My nephew shrugged and decided to ask around anyway.

What he learned was Blue Eye had come to the adopt-a-thon with the shelter. A volunteer said she'd somehow opened her crate and then bolted off into the rain earlier, and they'd been too busy to collect her.

"We should have known," the volunteer said, laughing. "She initially landed about three weeks ago at the shelter with her brother. Nobody really knows anything about them."

"Brother?" Charlie asked.

"Yes." The volunteer chuckled again. "It was quite a scene. About half an hour after the puppies were processed, she figured out how to let herself out of her crate. Then she opened his crate, too. And our surprised staff member on duty then watched her open the back door. Her brother ran out – and boy, is he fast! He disappeared before anyone could catch him."

"So nobody's seen him since?"

"That's right," she replied, her voice quieting. "But for some reason, she stayed. And we were hoping she could get adopted today. Or else she's going to be put down."

Charlie nodded. He teared up at the idea that, even though today was her last chance to find a forever home, the shelter staff was too preoccupied with other duties to make an adoption likely to happen.

He knew he had to find Blue Eye, so he thanked the volunteer and hurried into the rain. He hadn't gone 100 yards before movement near a cemetery gate across the road caught his eye. It was her! But now Blue Eye was moving slowly, her nose nudging a long-legged pup that was even more emaciated than she was. When she saw Charlie, Blue Eye barked and raced to meet him before darting back to her obviously weak companion. As Charlie scooped up this new little bag of bones, he knew one thing – some things are fated. And when Kismet comes calling, it's time to open the heart and surrender to what's meant to be.

As I stood listening to all that Charlie was sharing, tears kept dripping from my lashes. My heart kept whispering that, while I had a million excuses, I didn't have a single reason to turn my back on these puppies.

"Yes," I said at last.

"You mean – "

"Yes, Charlie," I repeated. "Let's do this."

"YES!" His voice bellowed high-five excitement. "I'll be there with your new fur kids in two days!"

A Fateful Meeting

Not quite 48 hours later, I heard a car pull up outside. Glancing at the framed words in my foyer – "Audentes fortuna adiuvat" – I affirmed my belief that fortune really does favor the bold as I stepped outside.

Not quite 10 minutes later, after Charlie and I had strategized on the best way to carry out this introduction, I found myself giggling on the grass. Two wriggly pups were licking and nipping and yipping as they tag teamed me onto my back. Then they proceeded to snuggle into me, one nestled under each arm. In moments, they were both sleeping.

"Can you believe it?" I asked, incredulous.

"Unbelievable," he replied. "So how are you feeling, Aunt Jean? Does it seem like they're meant to stay with you?"

"Some things are meant to be," I said. Looking at these emaciated bodies now resting so deeply – and that still were so eager to love – I started to cry. "This is one of them."

Crazily, Happily Ever After

It's been some time since Blue Eye and her brother came to live with me and my other two rescue dogs: Rosey, the basset mix, and Connell, the golden retriever mutt. It took a minute, but these four pups representing a whole United Nations of Breeds have become fur family. It took another minute, but names surfaced for this lovable, live-wire pair. Blue Eye became Kali-Ma, the primordial Hindu Mother-Goddess, in a nod to her black (and now shiny) coat and her deeply instinctive mothering ways. Her brother became Bodhi, since he has brought such enlightenment to our home through gentleness.

Yes, it's a struggle some days, but I always manage to laugh. Since landing at my door and in my heart, Kali has chewed up three pairs of shoes, many socks, and a box of matches; eaten sage and incense she pilfered from my desk; and enthusiastically dug about a dozen holes in the backyard. Not to be outdone, Bodhi has gnawed pieces out of my favorite foam roller, stolen and eaten a loaf of bread off the stove that I'd baked for company, and destroyed a fan's remote control.

Considering how painfully thin the puppies were when they arrived at my doorstep, I am grateful when anything gets chewed or eaten that their bellies are full – and at least they aren't eating out of desperation.

There are reminders of their hungry days "on the street." I'm convinced Bodhi devoured bugs to stay alive during the three weeks he was on his own after Kali-Ma let him out of the shelter. He eats any insect he finds in the house. For her part, Kali-Ma growls while her face is buried in her food bowl. It doesn't matter that none of the other dogs ever try to steal a morsel; she defends that dish! Perhaps, as time passes, the bug chasing and bowl growling will simply stop. Love has a way of doing that.

And love is really who these puppies are. Bodhi has such soft eyes, and when anyone pets him, he literally melts against that person. With Kali, there is sweet concern for others' well-being. If any of the other fur kids is having a bad moment – or if any of her human family is suffering for any reason – she plops herself down beside the one who's struggling and offers a lick and a snuggle.

In my wildest dreams, I never imagined adding two puppies to the mix of my life while big transitions and new beginnings were already at hand. Yet now I can't imagine life without them. Life without their sweet kisses and silly wrestling matches and soft nightly cuddles. Life without their absolutely unconditional love.

Together, we are going to be living crazily, happily ever after. All because fate stepped in and asked me to step up and open my heart just a bit deeper, just a bit wider. And in so doing, I see how saying "yes" to love affirms and allows in all the best life has to offer.

Love and Loss Action Steps

1. Take love one step further today. Offer just a bit more compassion. Offer an extra smile at work or at the store. Take that moment to offer a compliment that could have slipped by. Give yourself a touch more patience when dealing with a challenge.

2. Reflect on your circle. Is the "herd" of people around you a strong one? Do you build each other up? Bring yourself more happiness and positivity by giving your time to those that lift you up and in turn can be lifted up. Spending time with people that have positive common interests is a great way to start if you find you need or want to strengthen your herd. Also, see if it becomes clear who may need to be released from your circle if it is only negativity or drama you are receiving.

3. Sometimes in loss and grief, changing our environment and trying new experiences can uplift our spirits and help assuage feelings of sadness. If you live in the city, what about spending a day on a farm or ranch? If you live on a farm or ranch, how about a day in the city? See what it's like for the people and animals that live there. Pre-plan activities or volunteering that engage you with animals. Ride a horse. Milk a cow. Walk a dog in the city. What an adventure!

Affirmations

I strive to love people like my animals love me.
I deserve to love myself as much as my animals love me.
Even when I feel sad about a loss, it's because I am remembering all that made me happy.

Journal Prompts

Many of the stories in this book mention what people have learned from the animals in their lives, even when they have lost them. What are three things your animal connections have taught you about yourself or about life?

What messages of love and support might animals be sharing with you? Animals can present messages to you anywhere in your day or in nature. When you are walking, looking out a window, driving, or even in a dream, start noticing what messages animals might be sharing. Is their presence relevant to a situation in your life? Journal about these animals and the messages they might be sharing.

What's a relationship – with a person or animal – that caused your heart to open just a little bit more? Why do you think animals have such a great capacity to love us? Why do you think we have such a great capacity to love animals? How does this help our human relationships?

Animal Prints on My Soul Contributors

Joyce Benning is a born and bred country girl. Her passion is loving and caring for animals with a natural approach, along with inspiring others to live a Robust Lifestyle! Animals are not just in her life, they are her life! Groucho, her red heeler dog, is her very best buddy! He has taught her to never give up and live life with faith, not fear! Joyce is truly blessed to have amazing animal families in her life that make her world complete! She has two wonderful children that are a constant inspiration and help her hold her heart accountable.

Esta Bernstein is the founder of Saffyre Sanctuary, Inc., author of *Changing Horses*, and an equine intuitive counselor and nutritional consultant. She grew up in the racing industry with over 45 years of equine experience. Esta learned how to rehabilitate horses from her own horse, Caleyndar. After years of researching traditional methods to heal him, destiny brought her to racehorse nutritionist, Frank Lampley, whom she studied with for over 20 years. During that time, and even after the death of Frank, his supplement company refers clients to Esta for consultations for their most complex rehabilitation cases.

Author, acupuncturist, and non-profit founder *Jean Brannon* is committed to the Absolute Love Publishing philosophy – that of promoting goodness in this world. Whether she is writing, performing treatments, or rolling up her sleeves and helping the disadvantaged, Jean follows a path of service that helps to uplift and empower others. She and her four rescue pups live in southwestern Virginia. Jeanbrannon.com

Alexis Braswell is the horse team leader and riding instructor for The Red Barn in Leeds, Alabama. She has been riding horses since she was eight years old and has won many Alabama, United States, and world horse show competitions. She graduated from Birmingham-Southern College majoring in religion, with a psychology minor. She loves horses, horses, and working with children as they learn about horses.

Jo Dibblee is best known for her philanthropic work in Canada, the United States, and Mexico, and for being an animal lover. For as far back as she can remember, she has lived her life in service to animals and humans, with dogs at the center of that love. As a speaker and author of several international award-winning best-selling books, beginning with *Frock Off: Living Undisguised*, Jo shares how her rescue pup helped her untangle and heal. She shares her true story of being a key witness in hiding for 35 years in a murder investigation.

Sharon Dilley is a lifelong educator and animal lover. With her degree in elementary education, she has taken her decades of teaching into the realm of the K9 to teach dogs and their people how to elegantly navigate the human world. She has developed a groundbreaking schooling program built on connection, meeting the animal's needs, and regulating the environment that empowers young dogs to excel in any environment. Her expertise has served dogs and humans in search and rescue, veterans affairs, and everyday life. She lives in Oklahoma with her husband and her animals. Find her at www.the-puppypuzzle.com.

As an animal intuitive and clairvoyant, **Ginny Jablonski** helps animals and their caretakers understand how past trauma is affecting their lives. The experiences of her own life compelled her on a journey of exploring the Great Mystery of our true infinite nature. She employs all that she has learned on her own journey to self-awareness and self-responsibility with others. She calls her approach to assist others "compassionate wisdom." You can find out more information about Ginny and her work at www.heartofthehorse.us.

Katherine Jensen is a Pisces, a coat of many colors, and has been self-employed since she was 21 years old, having successfully built and sold three businesses. Now she is currently on the next chapter of her life. Motivating and inspiring people through her work is always her main objective. She is a professional life coach, dog trainer, and owner of two dogs, Storm and Odin. Her life has not been an easy one, but with a lot of study and self-love, she has achieved some of the most wonderful things. And you can too when you believe in yourself.

Kathy Lynn Mackison is the creator of the AWKWARDly Beautiful Life. After years of amazing results in her corporate career at an accounting firm, she finally realized that she was still unfulfilled and had lost herself. She woke up at age 45 realizing she had been living a life of hurry and worry. Kat Lynn sought coaching and returned to the Bible, the inspired Word of God. She found whole life balance (spirit, heart, mind, and body) and realized that her mission from heavenly Father was much bigger than to sit behind a desk for the rest of her life.

Deb Matlock grew up in the mountains of Colorado and is deeply committed to nurturing the connection between people, animals, earth, and spirit. She has spent 25 years working as a professional environmental educator, naturalist, and spiritual life coach. Deb holds a Master of Arts in environmental education from Prescott College and is pursuing her doctoral degree in environmental studies at Antioch University New England. Her research focus is integrating the more-than-human voice into nature connection work. You can reach her at www.wild-rhythms.com.

Daphne McDonagh is a rehabilitation and wellness practitioner who offers in-person and distance healing energy work for animals and people. She assists people to unwind from the stress and dis-ease of life. Daphne's sessions dissolve trapped energies and physical pain. Through the power of healing intent, along with sacred geometry tools, cold laser, and crystal therapy, Daphne sends healing vibrations anywhere in the world. She is an international best-selling author and a public speaker who has been interviewed on various international podcasts. She has a rehabilitation practitioner, animal sciences, and healing with crystals diploma.

Naomi McDonald is a former horse trainer. She is a certified shamanic practitioner who graduated from the Four Winds Society's Healing the Light Body School. She is an animal communicator and workshop presenter. In her workshops, she uses a unique combination of quantum physics, metaphysics, and the healing traditions of ancient medicine men and women to create powerful opportunities for self-discovery.

Ley-Anne Mountain is a licensed bodyworker, certified Death Doula, certified AFLCA Group Leader, and graduated with an animal health technology diploma. She also has completed multiple animal-assisted therapy courses including advanced craniosacral therapy and dolphin exploration, bringing interspecies craniosacral therapy sessions to her family's homestead. She received the Emerging Storyteller 2018 Scholarship.

Lorie Murphey was born into a large family in Oregon. She is number eight of nine and grew up camping, hunting, and fishing with her family. She loves the outdoors, and especially being in the mountains. She has one amazing daughter and a crazy love for Jesus and horses.

Kate Neligan is a best-selling author, an equine-partnered life/business coach, healer, and animal communicator devoted to the human-animal bond. She has been a TEDx speaker and writer for the Huffington Post. She pairs her intuitive gifts with those of horses and goats to help people access their own inner power and gifts. She has a master's in spiritual psychology and created Awakening With Equines. In her equine coaching sessions/workshops, Kate facilitates powerful transformation by helping high-performing women navigate life transitions with more ease, presence, and flow. She also supports companies in developing mindful cultures and communication skills. www.consciousrockstar.com

Donna Palamar holds a master's degree in educational leadership, management, and policy from Seton Hall University, and cherishes the journey of life, learning, and the pursuit of dark chocolate all over the world. She is an educator, author, international speaker, columnist, and coach. As The Menopause Fairy, Donna is a modern-day change agent who celebrates the magic, mystery, and mayhem of life, taking bold action to educate, celebrate and collaborate with women in all phases of life around the globe to heal, grow and "BE the best version of yourself possible!"

Beth Lauren Parrish is a certified Level 3 CHA Riding Instructor and Level I certified Equestrian Tai Chi Instructor. She has taught thousands of lessons for the past 20 years across the United States and now teaches worldwide remotely. With her business, Inspired Riding, Beth has created courses, meditations, the Focus app, and a journal for Inspired Riders to help them become more confident and connected with their horses. She teaches equestrians to trust their intuition and have conversations with their horses telepathically, which sets up each horse and rider to have the best co-creative dances possible.

Haseena Patel is an author, mind-body-spirit breakthrough coach, international speaker, yoga instructor, Akashic Records reader, and poet from South Africa. Through her proprietary UN-Becoming system she empowers individuals to break through their limits and live out their deepest truth. Haseena is co-founder of Leave No Girl Behind International, an organization that empowers girls worldwide through leadership programs. She is co-creator of the Bubbles Beyond Borders global campaign for gender equality which focuses on holding summits to build self-worth. Haseena loves connecting with her readers worldwide and can be reached via haseenapatel.com and leavenogirlbehind.org.

Marla Patrick is the owner of Smoky Valley Dog Center. She alternates living between her home on a farm near Lindsborg, Kansas, and her island home on Caye Caulker, Belize. In Marla's spare time, she grooms the island dogs in need at no cost, is an ambassador for the Beagle Freedom Project, collects supplies for the Caye Caulker Humane Society, and collects school supplies for the island's school children. She recently started collecting eyeglasses and hearing aids for the elderly of Caye Caulker. She lives with her husband, Jeff. They have three children, five grandchildren, three dogs, and two grand-dogs.

Angie Payne grew up with a deep love for horses and is the founder and practitioner at Equine Enrichment, which opened its doors in late 2012. One day a horse exposed Angie's demons and at that point, she remembered it being difficult to stuff that pain back inside. In early 2011 she spent two years becoming a certified Equine Gestalt Coach, learning to support others and do her deep difficult healing. Today, Angie has found her purpose and supports people who struggle with traumatic experiences in life, partnering with her horses. She can be found on Facebook at Equine Enrichment.

Tracy Pierce connects animal lovers to the thoughts and feelings of their animal friends so they can resolve pet problems and create more peace, harmony, and understanding at home. Tracy is an animal communicator based in Colorado. She is inspired to connect humans with the deeper wisdom of their animal friends through one-on-one animal communication sessions and animal communication workshops. Although she loves connecting with animals in person, most of her sessions are conducted virtually with clients around the world thanks to the magic of the internet. Learn more at tracy-pierce.com.

Linda Roberts is an animal lover who enjoys living with a variety of animals. It's through an energetic, heartfelt connection that she is able to acquire an understanding of the animal's thoughts, actions, and feelings. Linda enjoys helping people to solve the mysteries surrounding their animal behaviors and health concerns and teaching others about this natural ability. She enjoys the company of her two shelties, her two rescue cats, and her horse, Howie, who's health crisis led Linda to learn animal communication. Linda created Whispers of Love, Inc., her animal communication practice, to help to give animals a voice. www.thewhispersoflove.com

After accidentally rescuing a puppy 26 years ago, **Diane Rose-Solomon** became involved with animal rescue and adoption. She is a Certified Humane Education Specialist and the author of the award-winning children's books: *JJ the American Street Dog and How He Came to Live in Our House*, *JJ Goes to Puppy Class*, and *What to Expect When Adopting a Dog*, a non-fiction guide to successful dog adoption for every family. Her latest project, Animal Magic Films, shares the power of the human-animal-bond and the myriad therapeutic ways animals help people in a series of documentary films.

Stef Skupin (DVM, LVT, Owner & Facilitator at The Leaders Work) supports people in challenging careers such as healthcare to excel while maintaining a peaceful, relaxed mindset. Stef knows that stress, even in difficult situations, is an optional response. She believes that doctors and primary caregivers are more effective when they have the ability to stay relaxed at work. She loves watching the transformation of stress to inner peace and understanding in the people she works with, allowing them to reconnect with the passion for healing and supporting their patients. She also works as an animal communicator.

Abigail Stimpert is a 2016 graduate of Zion Academy. She chose not to attend college in order to commit her life to the farm. She enjoys hand milking her cows, organic gardening, and helping care for the family farm where she grew up in Southwest Kansas. She works in the huge gardens and cannery that support her family's gourmet pickle business. She loves cuddling with her family's German shepherds and her cat, Jack.

Hannah Stimpert is a 20-year-old homesteader who enjoys training and caring for her horse, Honey, her milk cows, chickens, and pets. She and her sister are the sixth generation on their 100 acres in Southwest Kansas. Most of her time is spent helping with her family's gourmet pickle business. She also enjoys baking pies for farmer's markets and running her small art business. She hopes someday to restore old trucks and bring them back to their former glory.

Candace Gish helps women open their eyes to the possibilities around them. As founder of the Divas That Care podcast community and network, Candace enjoys connecting with goal-oriented women committed to making a difference. She advocates for collaborative mentorship and strong, supportive groups of women converging to create change. Candace's four daughters and husband inspire her every day.

♡ a Divas That Care Collection

DivasThatCare.com

On behalf of Absolute Love Publishing and Divas
That Care, we hope you enjoyed

Animal Prints on My Soul

We'd love to see your online review anywhere books
are sold!

Please continue reading to browse additional
Absolute Love Publishing books. And, as always,
visit us at absolutelovepublishing.com, where you
can find free goodies, website exclusives, and more
info on all of our books and products.

ALOVEDLIFE

ALOVEDLIFE VOLUME 1 — AN ABSOLUTE LOVE PUBLISHING SPECIAL EDITION

Take Charge of Your WEALTH SIGNATURE

What Is Your Resonant FREQUENCY?

Shiny Object Syndrome: Clear the Path to Your HIGHER PURPOSE

AMPLIFY YOUR WHY

GRATITUDE: Deepen Your Relationship

HALOTHERAPY: Use Salt to Heal Your Body

CONSCIOUSLY CREATE A LIFE YOU LOVE

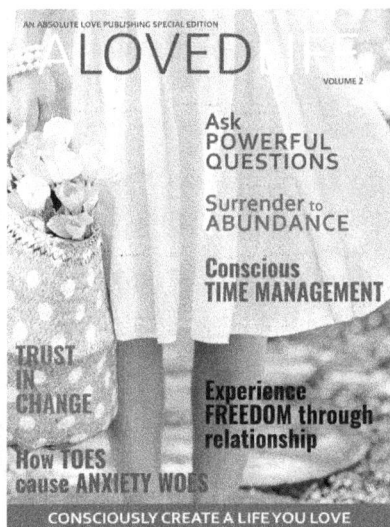

ALOVED VOLUME 2 — AN ABSOLUTE LOVE PUBLISHING SPECIAL EDITION

Ask POWERFUL QUESTIONS

Surrender to ABUNDANCE

Conscious TIME MANAGEMENT

TRUST IN CHANGE

Experience FREEDOM through relationship

How TOES cause ANXIETY WOES

CONSCIOUSLY CREATE A LIFE YOU LOVE

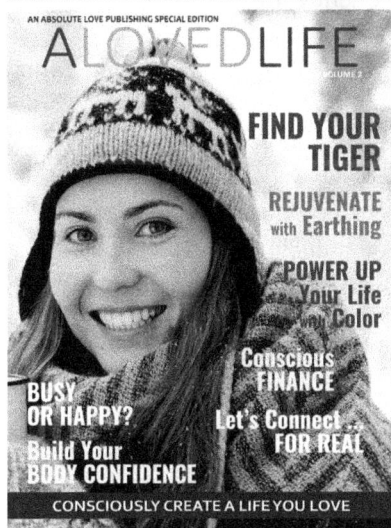

ALOVEDLIFE VOLUME 3 — AN ABSOLUTE LOVE PUBLISHING SPECIAL EDITION

FIND YOUR TIGER

REJUVENATE with Earthing

POWER UP Your Life with Color

Conscious FINANCE

BUSY OR HAPPY?

Let's Connect ... FOR REAL

Build Your BODY CONFIDENCE

CONSCIOUSLY CREATE A LIFE YOU LOVE

ALOVEDLIFE VOLUME 4 — AN ABSOLUTE LOVE PUBLISHING SPECIAL EDITION

Release Expectations

CONNECT with Your Higher Purpose

FOLLOW Your FUN

Use Sound to UPLIFT Your Life

What Your Symptoms are Saying

WHAT'S LOVE GOT TO DO WITH IT?

CONSCIOUSLY CREATE A LIFE YOU LOVE

Consciously create a life you love with ALOVEDLIFE. This booka-zine by Absolute Love Publishing features stories on Intentional Living, Elevated Action, Conscious Connection, and Sacred Self Care. And because it's timeless (meaning, you can read each volume at any time,) jump in or catch up any way you'd like! Collect them all to read again and again. Find all available editions and formats at www.absolutelovepublishing.com/shop.

Raise Your Vibration
Min-e-book™ Series
by Caroline A. Shearer

Raise Your Vibration: Tips and Tools for a High-Frequency Life

Presenting mind-opening concepts and tips, *Raise Your Vibration* opens the doorway to your highest and greatest good! This min-e-book™ demonstrates how every thought and every action affect our level of attraction, enabling us to attain what we truly want in life. As beings of energy that give off and respond to vibration, it's important we understand the clarity, fullness, and happiness that come from living at a higher frequency. Divided into categories of mind, body, and spirit/soul, readers will learn practical steps they immediately can put into practice to resonate at a higher vibration and to further evolve their souls. A must-read primer for a higher existence! Are you ready for a high-frequency life?

Raise Your Financial Vibration: Tips and Tools to Embrace Your Infinite Spiritual Abundance

Are you ready to release the mind dramas that hold you back from your infinite spiritual abundance? Are you ready for a high-frequency financial life? Allow, embrace, and enjoy your infinite spiritual abundance and financial wealth today! Absolute Love Publishing Creator Caroline A. Shearer explores simple steps and shifts in mindset that will help you receive the abundance you desire in *Raise Your Financial Vibration*. Learn how to release blocks to financial abundance, create thought patterns that will help you achieve a more desirable financial reality, and fully step into an abundant lifestyle by discovering the art of being abundant.

Raise Your Verbal Vibration: Create the Life You Want with Law of Attraction Language

Are the words you speak bringing you closer to the life you want? Or are your word choices inadvertently creating more difficulties? Discover words and phrases that are part of the Language of Light in Caroline A. Shearer's latest in the Raise Your Vibration min-e-book™ series: *Raise Your Verbal Vibration*. Learn what common phrases and words may be holding you back, and utilize a list of high-vibration words that you can begin to incorporate into your vocabulary. Increase your verbal vibration today with this compelling addition to the Raise Your Vibration series!

Metaphysical Fiction

Atlantis Writhing
by Jean Brannon

Bronze winner of the COVR Visionary Awards
A civilization trembling toward collapse—
and the unbreakable love that may bring
Atlantis back from the brink. Atlantis is writhing. Chaos and greed have
granted an obsessive new monarch enough power to destroy the world—
and beyond. The only thing standing between King Gadeirus and inter-
galactic annihilation is Elysia and her fellow Light Ray missionaries. As
time grows short, the missionaries work to overcome the evil Lesser Light
forces. When all options have been stripped away, a symbol long lost to
antiquity surfaces just in time to inspire them to concoct one last desper-
ate scheme. Forbidden longings must be dealt with, too. Cravings Elysia
must confront in the presence of hypnotic Alaric, a visiting dignitary with
a scandalous past. But behind his seductive ways is a shocking secret—an
unexpected key that may help Elysia unlock her potent power and wield it
in the fight for the Highest Light.

Dead End Date
by Caroline A. Shearer

Dead End Date is the first book in a meta-
physical series about a woman's crusade to
teach the world about love, one mystery and
personal hang-up at a time. In a Bridget Jones meets New Age-style, *Dead
End Date* introduces readers to Faith, a young woman whose dating disasters and personal angst have separated her from the reason she's on Earth.
When she receives the shocking news that she is a lightworker and has
one year to fulfill her life purpose, Faith embarks on her mission with zeal,
tackling problems big and small—including the death of her blind date.
Working with angels and psychic abilities and even the murder victim
himself, Faith dives headfirst into a personal journey that will transform
all those around her and, eventually, all those around the world.

Self-Help

Have Your Cake and Be Happy, Too: A Joyful Approach to Weight Loss
by Michelle Hastie

Have you tried every weight loss trick and diet out there only to still feel stuck with unwanted body fat? Are you ready to live joyfully and fully, in a body that stores only the amount of fat it needs? Then this book is for you. In *Have Your Cake and Eat It, Too: A Joyful Approach to Weight Loss*, author Michelle Hastie uses her own research into nutrition and the psychology of weight loss to help you uncover the mindset you need to transition from fat storing to fat burning, without overly fancy or external tactics. No more strict regimens or unfulfilling meals. Just strong body awareness, deep mind-body connection, and positive results. Don't change your diet or your exercise routine. Instead, pick up this book, and change your life.

The Weight Loss Shift: Be More, Weigh Less
by Michelle Hastie

The Weight Loss Shift: Be More, Weigh Less by Michelle Hastie helps those searching for their ideal bodies shift into a higher way of being, inviting the lasting weight they want—along with the life of their dreams! Skip the diets and the gimmicks, *The Weight Loss Shift* is a permanent weight loss solution. Based on science, psychology, and spirituality, Hastie helps readers discover their ideal way of being through detailed instructions and exercises, and then helps readers transform to living a life free from worry about weight—forever! Would you like to love your body at any weight? Would you like to filter through others' body expectations to discover your own? Would you like to live at your ideal weight naturally, effortlessly, and happily? Then make the shift with *The Weight Loss Shift: Be More, Weigh Less!*

Mom Humor

Mom Life: Perfection Pending
by Meredith Ethington

Out-parented at PTA? Out-liked on social media? Wondering how your best friend from high school's kids are always color-coordinated, angelic, and beaming from every photo, while your kids look more like feral monkeys? It's okay. Imperfection is the new perfection! Join Meredith Ethington, "one of the funniest parents on Facebook," according to Today.com, as she relates encouraging stories of real-mom life in her debut parenting humor book, *Mom Life: Perfection Pending.*

Whether you're buried in piles of laundry, packing your 50th sack lunch for the week, or almost making it out the door in time for school, you'll laugh along with stories of what real-mom life is like—and realize that sometimes simply making it through the day is good enough. An uplifting yet real look at all that is expected of moms in the 21st century, *Mom Life* is so relatable you'll find yourself saying, "I guess I'm doing okay after all."

How-to

Preparing to Fly: Financial Freedom from Domestic Abuse
by Sarah Hackley

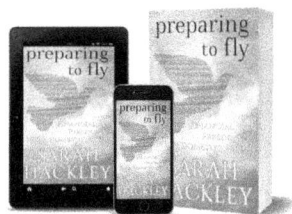

Are financial worries keeping you stuck in an abusive or unhealthy relationship? Do you want to break free but don't know how to make it work financially? Take charge with *Preparing to Fly*, a personal finance book for women who want to escape the relationships that are holding them back. Drawing on personal experiences and nearly a decade of financial expertise, Sarah Hackley walks readers step-by-step through empowering plans and tools: Learn how much money it will take to leave and how much you'll need to live on your own. Change the way you think about money to promote your independence. Bring control of your life back to where it belongs—with you. Break free and live in your own power, with *Preparing to Fly*.

Anthologies & Guides

Love Like God: Embracing Unconditional Love

In this groundbreaking compilation, well-known individuals from across the globe share stories of how they learned to release the conditions that block absolute love. Along with the insights of best-selling author Caroline A. Shearer, readers will be reminded of their natural state of love and will begin to envision a world without fear or judgement or pain. Along with Shearer's reflections and affirmations, experts, musicians, authors, professional athletes, and others shed light on the universal experiences of journeying the path of unconditional love.

Love Like God Companion Book

You've read the love-expanding essays from the luminaries of *Love Like God*. Now, take your love steps further with the *Love Like God Companion Book*. The Companion provides a positive, actionable pathway into a state of absolute love, enabling readers to further open their hearts at a pace that matches their experiences. This book features an expanded introduction, the Thoughts and Affirmations from *Love Like God*, plus all new "Love in Action Steps."

Women Will Save the World

Leading women across the nation celebrate the feminine nature through stories of collaboration, creativity, intuition, nurturing, strength, trailblazing, and wisdom in *Women Will Save the World*. Inspired by a quote from the Dalai Lama, bestselling author and Absolute Love Publishing Founder Caroline A. Shearer brings these inherent feminine qualities to the forefront, inviting a discussion of the impact women have on humanity and initiating the question: Will women save the world?

Animal Prints on My Soul
by Candace Gish

Animals can be our heroes, our confidantes, our coaches, and our best examples of unconditional love. In *Animal Prints on My Soul*, we explore the human-animal bond through the experiences and stories of women. Featuring horses, dogs, cats, birds, and more, animal lovers will connect with these ordinary – yet extraordinary – stories of how animals impact our lives. Heartwarming, touching, and joyful, this book is a splendid gift for those who love animals. The stories of Healing, Connection, and Love & Loss also encourage us to pause and appreciate the wonderful gifts our animal friends bring us so we've provided deeper-dive prompts for those who would like to transform these blessings into inspiration for their own lives.

Min-e-books™

The Chakra Secret: What Your Body Is Telling You
by Michelle Hastie

Do you believe there may be more to the body than meets the eye? Have you wondered why you run into the same physical issues over and over again? Maybe you are dealing with dis-eases or ailments and are ready to treat more than just the symptoms. Or perhaps you've simply wondered why you gain weight in your midsection while your friend gains weight in her hips? Get ready to understand how powerful energy centers in your body communicate messages from beyond the physical. Discover the root, energetic problems that are causing imbalances, and harness a universal power to create drastic changes in your happiness, your well-being, and your body with *The Chakra Secret*.

Finding Happiness with Migraines: a Do It Yourself Guide
by Sarah Hackley

Do you have monthly, weekly, or even daily migraines? Do you feel lonely or isolated, or like you are constantly worrying about the next impending migraine attack? Is the weight of living with migraine disease dampening your enjoyment of the "now"? Experience the happiness you crave with *Finding Happiness with Migraines*. Discover how you can take charge of your body, your mind, your emotions, and your health by practicing simple, achievable steps that create a daily life filled with more joy, appreciation, and confidence. Sarah's Five Steps to Finding Happiness with Migraines provide an actionable path to a new, happier way of living with migraine disease. A few of the tools you'll learn: which yoga poses can help with a migraine attack, why you should throw away your daily migraine journal, how do-it-yourself therapy can create positive change, and techniques to connect with your body and intuition.

Pants Down: How the Trousers-to Toes Chakras Can Keep You Turned on, Tuned in, And Toned up
by Jean Brannon

Licensed acupuncturist Jean Brannon explores the fascinating connection between little-known lower body chakras and our self-limiting beliefs in *Pants Down*. In this min-e-book™, dive deeper than the well-known seven chakras to discover how these powerful energy centers can help you live in a turned on, tuned in, and toned up kind of way. Using ancient tools from Buddhism and Hinduism, as well as modern brain science, Brannon shares the tips and tools she has developed during more than 20 years of clinical practice to help you break through these constricted beliefs and live a more expansive life.

- Examine how the lower body chakras have evolved and how they affect us
- Learn how emotion and memory can cause unwanted behaviors
- Discover how to tap into and balance the trousers-to-toes chakras for a greater sense of well-being

Get turned on, tuned in, and toned up today with *Pants Down*!

Where Is the Gift? Discovering the Blessing in Every Situation
by Caroline A. Shearer

Inside every challenge is a beautiful blessing waiting for us to unwrap it. All it takes is our choice to learn the lesson of the challenge! Are you in a situation that is challenging you? Are you struggling with finding the perfect blessing the universe is holding for you? This min-e-book™ will help you unwrap your blessings with more ease and grace, trust in the perfect manifestation of your life's challenges, and move through life with the smooth path your higher self intended. Make the choice: unwrap your gift today!

Middle Grade
and Young Adult Books

Different
by Janet McLaughlin

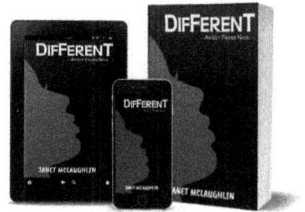

An Amelia Island Book Festival selection
Twelve-year-old Izzy wants to be like everyone else, but she has a secret. She isn't weird or angry, like some of the kids at school think. Izzy has Tourette syndrome. Hiding outbursts and tics from her classmates is hard enough, but when a new girl arrives, Izzy's fear of losing her best friend makes Izzy's symptoms worse. And when she sees her crush act suspiciously, runaway thoughts take root inside of her. As the pressure builds and her world threatens to spin out of control, Izzy must face her fear and reveal her secret, whatever the costs.

Authentic and perceptive, *Different* shines a light on the delicate line of a child's hopes and fears and inspires us all to believe that perhaps we are not so different after all.

The Adima Chronicles by Steve Schatz

Adima Rising

For millennia, the evil Kroledutz have fed on the essence of humans and clashed in secret with the Adima, the light weavers of the universe. Now, with the balance of power shifting toward darkness, time is running out. Guided by a timeless Native American spirit, four teenagers from a small New Mexico town discover they have one month to awaken their inner power and save the world. Rory, Tima, Billy, and James must solve four ancient challenges by the next full moon to awaken a mystical portal and become Adima. If they fail, the last threads of light will dissolve, and the universe will be lost forever. Can they put aside their fears and discover their true natures before it's too late?

Adima Returning

The Sacred Cliff is crumbling and with it the Adima way of life! Weakened by the absence of their beloved friend James, Rory, Tima, and Billy must battle time and unseen forces to unite the greatest powers of all dimensions in one goal. They must move the Sacred Cliff before it traps all Adima on Earth—and apart from the primal energy of the Spheres—forever!

Aided by a surprising and timeless maiden, the three light-weaving teens travel across the planes of existence to gain help from the magical creatures who guard the Adima's most powerful objects, the Olohos. There is only one path to success: convince the guardians to help. Fail and the Cliff dissolves, destroying the once-eternal Spheres and the interdimensional light weavers known as Adima.

Like the exciting adventures of *Adima Rising*, the second spellbinding book of The Adima Chronicles will have your senses reeling up until its across-worlds climax. Will conscious creation and the bonds of friendship be enough to fight off destructive forces and save the world once again?

The Soul Sight Mysteries by Janet McLaughlin

Haunted Echo

Sun, fun, toes in the sand, and daydreams about her boyfriend back home. That's what teen psychic Zoey Christopher expects for her spring break on an exotic island. But from the moment she steps foot onto her best friend Becca's property, Zoey realizes the island has other plans: chilling drum beats, a shadowy ghost, and a mysterious voodoo doll. Zoey has always seen visions of the future, but when she arrives at St. Anthony's Island to vacation among the jet set, she has her first encounter with a bona fide ghost. Forced to uncover the secret behind the girl's untimely death, Zoey quickly realizes that trying to solve the case will thrust her into mortal danger—and into the arms of a budding crush. Can Zoey put the tormented spirit's soul to rest without her own wild emotions haunting her?

Fireworks

Dreams aren't real. Psychic teen Zoey Christopher knows the difference between dreams and visions better than anyone, but ever since she and her best friend returned from spring vacation, Zoey's dreams have been warning her that Becca is in danger. But a dream isn't a vision—right? Besides, Zoey has other things to worry about, like the new, cute boy in school. Dan obviously has something to hide, and he won't leave Zoey alone—even when it causes major problems with Josh, Zoey's boyfriend. Is it possible he knows her secret?

Then, one night, Becca doesn't answer any of Zoey's texts or calls. She doesn't answer the next morning either. When Zoey's worst fears come true, her only choice is to turn to Dan, whom she discovers has a gift different from her own but just as powerful. Is it fate? Will using their gifts together help them save Becca, or will the darkness win? Discover what's real and what's just a dream in *Fireworks*!

Serafina Loves Science! by Cara Bartek

Cosmic Conundrum

Sixth grader Serafina Sterling finds herself accepted into the Ivy League of space adventures for commercial astronauts, where she'll study with Jeronimo Musgrave, a famous and flamboyant scientist who brought jet-engine minivans to the suburbs. Unfortunately, Serafina also meets Ida Hammer, a 12-year-old superstar of science who has her own theorem, a Nobel-Prize-winning mother, impeccable fashion sense—and a million social media followers. Basically, she's everything Serafina's not. Or so Serafina thinks. Even in an anti-gravity chamber, Serafina realizes surviving junior astronaut training will take more than just a thorough understanding of Newton's Laws. She'll have to conquer her fear of public speaking, stick to the rules, and overcome the antics of Ida. How will Serafina survive this cosmic conundrum?

Quantum Quagmire

Serafina suspects something is wrong when her best friend, Tori Copper, loses interest in their most cherished hobbies: bug hunting and pizza nights. When she learns Tori's parents are getting a divorce and that Tori's mom is moving away, Serafina vows to discover a scientific solution to a very personal problem so that Tori can be happy again. But will the scientific method, a clever plan, and a small army of arachnids be enough to reunite Tori's parents? When the situation goes haywire, Serafina realizes she has overlooked the smallest, most quantum of details. Will love be the one challenge science can't solve? Join Serafina in another endearing adventure in book two of the Serafina Loves Science! series.

www.ingramcontent.com/pod-product-compliance
Lightning Source LLC
Chambersburg PA
CBHW072151090426
42740CB00012B/2218